For Rashid and ~~Shannon~~ Megan,

Household Baggage

THE Moving Life OF A Soldier's Wife

Best wishes in your life together – either in or out of the Air Force!

Marna A. Krajeski

Marna A. Krajeski
Oct 06

Wyatt-MacKenzie Publishing, Inc.
DEADWOOD, OREGON

Household Baggage: The Moving Life of a Soldier's Wife
by Marna A. Krajeski

ISBN: 1-932279-28-8

Library of Congress Control Number: 2006925632

Published by The Mom-Writers Publishing Cooperative
Wyatt-MacKenzie Publishing, Inc., Deadwood, OR
www.WyMacPublishing.com (541) 964-3314

Requests for permission or further information should be addressed to:
Wyatt-MacKenzie Publishing
15115 Highway 36, Deadwood, Oregon 97430

Printed in the United States of America

Dedication

To Paul, my go-to guy, a good sport,
and the reason for it all to be.

Foreword

Army life is unique to say the least. The subculture, with its own language, rules, acronyms, and ways, is foreign to the general civilian population.

The Global War on Terrorism has brought more awareness and certainly more curiosity about Army life. Soldiers and their families have been thrust into the spotlight like never before.

Household Baggage offers timely and rare glimpses of Army life from the mid-80's to the present. Marna captures what it's like to be the spouse of a Soldier in today's Army. Her amusing and heartfelt vignettes are told with humor, poignancy, and pride. Marna writes about things we have all experienced, thought, obsessed about, and worried about. She makes us feel we are not alone, that we all have the same feelings and concerns.

Civilians will enjoy this book and gain a new appreciation for Soldiers, their families, and the sacrifices they make for our country. Military wives will identify with and love each and every chapter. This book makes you proud to be part of a very special sisterhood called Army Wives.

Vicki Cody
Army wife, Army mom, and author of
Your Soldier, Your Army: A Parents' Guide.

Song of a Military Wife

You don't need me anymore, do you? he said.
No, I don't need you.

I can clean the gutters, change the oil, shovel the driveway,
paint the bedroom, hang the curtains, grill the steaks.
I can mow the grass, trim the hedges, jumpstart the car,
clear the clog, fix the dryer, balance the checkbook.
I can stack wood, switch fuses, put up icicle lights,
coach soccer, play goalie, throw fast pitches.

I can, I can, I can
do it all while you're gone.
It sure was hard
to learn I didn't need you.
Welcome home.

Contents

Introduction

When Paul and I entered the Army in 1985, jungle fatigues were still an acceptable uniform. Documents were produced on electric typewriters, and smoking was permitted in government buildings. Memos thumb-tacked to the unit bulletin board were the equivalent of email. Although it's hard to believe in today's era of identity theft, my Social Security number was printed on my personal checks, and I even wrote it in block letters on my duffel bag for all to see.

Back then, the Berlin Wall separated West and East Germany. Ronald Reagan was president, and the U.S. was locked in a tense Cold War with the Soviet Union. The threat of nuclear destruction weighed on our minds.

I was a twenty-two year old graduate of the College of William and Mary. While attending on an ROTC scholarship, the training officer in the Military Science department asked about my eyesight.

"Practically bionic," I answered.

"Then you should try to go to flight school," he said.

That's how I ended up at Fort Rucker, Alabama, after college. With the Aviation Officer Basic Course and Initial Entry Rotary Wing training, I stayed there a year. I was later assigned to Hunter Army Airfield in Savannah, Georgia, where I flew the UH-1 (Huey) helicopter for five years in support of Fort Stewart.

Hunter was also the home of the 1st Ranger Battalion, a very impressive outfit to those of us who saw them around post. One evening friends introduced me to a tall, handsome ranger lieutenant with striking hazel eyes. We dated for a year and married in June 1989 at the Cathedral of St. John the Baptist in downtown Savannah.

Our plans included having a family, but I didn't think we

would succeed as a dual military couple with children. I had watched friends struggle with those multiple responsibilities. They dropped off their drowsy toddlers at the Child Development Center at 6 a.m. before dashing to morning formation. If alerts were called in the middle of the night, they scrambled for a babysitter. Field exercises required a grandparent or other full-time caregiver to provide coverage. It looked pretty stressful to me, and I knew I couldn't handle the conflicting commitments. When my five year service ended, I left active duty.

Paul and I then moved to Fort Myer, Virginia, where we had a baby daughter—Elena Kathleen. Assignments to Florida, New York, Kansas, Tennessee, and Rhode Island followed over the next decade. Our second child, Stephen Ashburn, was born in 1994.

During Elena's first year, I began writing columns about the military lifestyle.

After several of my essays had been published in the *Army Times* and other periodicals, I believed I had the beginnings of a collection.

For a Christmas present in 1997, Paul sent me on a weekend getaway, where I sketched out this work and brainstormed the title. "Household Baggage" is the Army term for everything you own, boxed up and loaded into a moving van. Although the contemporary synonym is "Household Goods," I think the earlier version is much more fitting.

When I returned after my short break, I told Paul, "I'm going to write the definitive book about being a military wife." As the manuscript progressed, I realized that trying to speak for every woman was impossible, but if I wrote honestly and openly about my experiences, I might ignite insights in other wives. When I'd received reader mail in the past, the most gratifying comment was, "Thank you for your article. I thought I was the only one who felt that way." Touching that common nerve became my goal.

Conversations with other military moms at playgrounds and meetings generated story ideas which I hastily scribbled on the back of commissary receipts. My minivan was littered with scraps of paper, clippings, and handwritten drafts. The notes and outlines for this project have been stowed and shipped more times than I care to count. With each move, I carefully unpacked the bulging files and binders from a box labeled "Household Baggage." Three computer upgrades, four duty stations, and ten years of interruptions later, my glimmer of an idea became reality.

Folks in the Army often say, "The more things change, the more they stay the same." Maps have altered since 1985. Germany has re-unified. "Soviet" is an historical term now, and we have new place names—Kazakhstan, Uzbekistan, etc. With the Global War on Terror, we've seen an unprecedented mobilization of Active Duty and Reserve forces. Our country faces threats to our security like never before. Yet at the heart of every military struggle, there's a human component. The emotional themes of marriage, parenting, and relocation remain constant for soldiers and spouses. *Household Baggage* isn't the definitive reference on military life; it's what happened to me over the past twenty years and what I think it means. C.S. Lewis once said, "We read to know we are not alone." If you are a military wife and you recognize yourself in these pages, please take comfort in the company.

As the Infantry says, "See you on the high ground."
Marna A. Krajeski
March 2006

Moving

Moving is a fundamental feature of the military and major life stressor. The title of this book—*Household Baggage*—is the term for a semi-truck's worth of furniture and belongings. In sixteen years of marriage, my family and I—husband Paul, children Stephen and Elena—have lived in ten places. As a result, I've barely kept my sanity as I sorted logistics, counted the children and pets, tracked down missing boxes, and settled in a new place.

Permanent-Change-of-Station Pandemonium

There is a type of woman, a "perfect" woman, who handles a permanent-change-of-station move with grace and composure. In her size six, pressed shorts (worn with panty hose), stylish flats, chic haircut, and glossed lips, she sips freshly brewed coffee while checking off the boxes being marched into her quarters. Her sweet children—two darling little girls who are best friends—play dolls in the back yard. Within seventy-two hours, the perfect military wife has stacked the flattened boxes at the curb, hung the pictures, stocked the kitchen, and planted petunias in the window boxes.

Naturally, I don't like her one bit.

Three days after the delivery of *our* household goods, I'm still lying flat-out with a cold compress plastered on my forehead. The house is a confusing heap of boxes, and the pizza man, who I already know by name, will be delivering dinner at any minute. I can't even find my purse.

Instead of being efficient and organized when we move, I choose to whine and complain. I find it to be a much more satisfying outlet for my tension.

On the drive from our last duty station, Baby Stephen developed an ear infection. He just wanted to be held and he cried constantly. None of us had had a decent night's sleep in a week. When the moving van arrived with our household baggage, I hoisted him on my hip and winced. My back, killing me after all the lousy hotel beds and the interruption in my exercise routine, seemed about to give way.

At 10 a.m. the man on the radio announced that the day was going to be "a scorcher. We're looking at record-high heat folks." Already it felt like a hundred degrees. The movers unloaded half a dozen boxes marked "Sweaters." I couldn't deal with the concept of wool. I couldn't even breathe. Right before I passed out, I shouted, "Put the boxes back in the van!" When I opened my eyes, my husband Paul was standing there. I snarled at him. "Nice of you to come back from in-processing." I handed him the moist baby. "By the way," I asked, "have you seen our daughter?"

"She's over there telling everyone what a mean mommy she has," he said, eyeing me warily. The steady diet of cheeseburgers and fries had padded me with an extra ten pounds. The only clothes that fit were a pair of cut-offs and a t-shirt that read, "Virginia is for Lovers." I wasn't in Virginia, certainly. But I was in desperate need of a haircut and highlight. They don't let women that look like me into the commissary.

I shot Paul a look that I hoped reminded him why we don't keep firearms in the house. At that moment I didn't like this life. I didn't like these quarters. I wasn't even sure I liked *him* anymore.

I've moved enough to know that these beastly moods pass. In time, my household would be organized, my children healthy, and my husband and I on speaking terms. Right then, however, the perfect military wife was MIA. She wanted air conditioning and a long nap.

Climate Shock

I think families should get a clothing allowance when the military moves them from a hot southern assignment to a cold northern one. We've done it twice: once from Florida to New York, another time from Tennessee to Rhode Island. Both times we had to retool our wardrobes to get through the first winter, spending a fortune in the process.

When Paul attended graduate school in Tallahassee, his duty uniform consisted of shorts and sandals. The city was a paradise lined with palm trees. In the spring, purple wisteria hung from the doorways and gardenia scented the air. The summers were hot, so hot that we had to spend three lazy months around the swimming pool. It was tough.

And the winters were mild too. In February of 1994 I was driving to my friend Pam's house. The radio was tuned to a syndicated talk show, and people were calling from all over the country to report their weather. "Minus forty degrees in South Dakota," ". . . snow and ice in Virginia," "Massachusetts schools closed again . . . ." Most of the country, it seemed, was frozen solid. I wore a cotton t-shirt, and with the car windows down and the sun roof open, I was still sweating. For a moment, I felt a pang of guilt. Then I realized I was just thirsty, so I stopped for a cold Coke.

That year I sent a cartoon to my friends living in colder climates. The caption read "As the weather outside / gets horrider and horrider / it's nice to say / I live in Florider."

After we moved to West Point, it didn't take long for that bad karma to come back around. Cold winds from the Hudson River felt like they were straight off the Arctic tundra. It snowed before Thanksgiving. The old timers saw that as a bad sign. Velour hoodies weren't going to get me through the winter.

Paul held up a black woolen coat from his cadet days and a pair of army boots.

"This is all I need," he said. I had lived in warm places for so long—Virginia, Alabama, Georgia, and Florida—that I didn't have a parka to my name. The children had no foul weather gear at all. Our kindergartner, Elena, had spent her life south of the Mason-Dixon line. Baby Stephen had worn undershirts and diapers since his birth in Tallahassee.

I immediately hit up the PX for something down-filled. In the picked-over merchandise I discovered one snowsuit for an eighteen-month old and a pair of ski mittens for me.

"Where are you going?" Paul asked, as I prepared to leave bright and early the next day.

"Off to the mall to buy winter stuff for everyone," I said.

I came home with coats for Elena and me. She didn't like hers, so I put it in the return pile, and we ordered a different one from the Hanna Andersson catalogue. We also bought the matching accessories. I was melting down the MasterCard and had only just begun.

"Shopping again?" Paul asked a few days later.

"I'm not through the first layer yet," I replied. "Today I'm buying hats, gloves, and scarves for the three of us. If there's time I'll get snow pants, warm socks, long underwear, and face masks for sledding," I said, reading off my list as I rushed past him.

"How much is all this costing?"

"Don't ask," I said. "By the way, can you stash those boxes of sun dresses and tank tops in the basement?"

When I got home, I heaved a shopping bag full of insulated boots at Paul before dashing off.

"Mary says there's a new shipment of turtlenecks at the PX. I've got to get down there before they sell out," I said. "Tomorrow I'll hit the coat sale at Filene's."

"You already have a winter coat," he reminded me.

"That's a casual one," I said. "I can't wear that to church. I need a long one for dressy occasions, and a scarf and hat to go with it."

Noting the look on his face, I added, "After that, we'll inventory to see what we're missing. I'm thinking sweaters and wool pants for starters. Maybe fleece playsuits for the baby. We're digging in for the winter."

Right before New Year's, weather reports warned of an ominous storm approaching. Cadets and faculty boomeranged back early from Christmas break, but many weren't quick enough. They got stranded in airports, unable to fly into the nearby New York airports.

The blizzard of 1996 dumped twenty-four inches of snow overnight. We couldn't move our cars for days. Finally, after almost a week of immobility, a front loader showed up and dug us out. The job was too big for a plow.

After the road was cleared, we were left with eight-foot mounds of snow in the front yard. Elena and her friends carved out an amazing kiddy slide which had to be mounted from steps made of garden timbers. We also had igloos and forts and mazes and a whole platoon of snowmen.

Bundled up in her new coat, Elena frolicked in the snow like a bear cub all day. Stephen, newly walking, was happy to be pulled in his "Baby 'Boggan," a deep sled that I got at the local hardware store.

With twilight beckoning one evening, I called for Elena. She leaned around the tree. Her nose was runny and her cheeks were red, but her hazel eyes were shining with delight.

"Don't make me come inside," she pleaded.

I gazed at my Nordic princess. Before I had even gotten the credit card bill for those winter clothes, she had become a bona fide blizzard kid.

"Five more minutes," I said. "The snow will be there tomorrow."

Curtain Calls

Once we've unpacked the kitchen, assembled the beds, arranged the furniture, and flattened the cardboard boxes, I hang curtains. This is always my first stab at decorating after we've moved into a new house. Like many military wives, I own dozens of valances and enough curtain rods to start a scrap metal yard.

My friend Angela never parts with window treatments, however dated or quirky they are. "You just never know when you'll need them again," she says. With each move, she carefully folds the curtains and zips them into huge plastic comforter bags. At last count, her collection had swelled to three stuffed sacks. After seventeen years as a military wife, she has a contingency plan for every window known to mankind. French doors? No problem. Oddball opening at the end of the hallway? Got the perfect swag. Basement porthole? Easy. Movie screen sized pane? No sweat. She's a master blaster window dresser.

Getting qualified as a combat window decorator took several moves. I started out with nothing, not even a mini-blind to my name, but I quickly caught on. My mother had taught me to sew, and I could create a shade out of a pillowcase.

At one house, the front room had an oversized picture window, far wider than any of my curtain sets. The sheers on it were yellowed, so I asked the landlord if I could take them down. He and his wife still had white shag carpeting and orange couches in their house, so they didn't quite understand my urgency, but they agreed. I decided to make a scalloped valance to go with my burgundy couch.

I bought eleven yards of floral chintz on sale. When I got home, I unrolled the bolt on the floor. The fabric spread diagonally from my front door, through the living room, and halfway across the dining room. It looked like the aisle runner at a wedding.

The house became my workroom. I sewed seams, stitched casings and hems, then attached shirring tape. It sounds pretty simple, except that I had so much fabric, I had to crawl around on my hands and knees for hours.

"When are you going to finish?" Paul shouted from the bedroom, where he had barricaded our four year old, Hurricane Elena. I heard Stephen in his crib whining "Ma-ma-ma-ma," which was baby-speak for "I want to teethe on the pin cushion."

"If I ever get the brilliant idea to do this again," I replied, "just shoot me."

"Yeah right, Martha Stewart," he said. "I've heard that before."

In the end, it was worthwhile. My softly gathered valance made an elegant and beautiful accessory. I've used it in five homes. It has decorated dining rooms and living rooms. Once I ripped apart the center seam and used it on two separate windows. Rejoined, it hung in our solarium, an unusual room with an entire wall of glass panes. As we threaded the valance onto a rod, our landlord asked if I had purchased the curtain especially for that room.

"No, I already had it," I said.

He walked away, muttering "No one owns curtains that are forty-five feet wide." He had never leased to a military family.

Our rental was a three-bedroom house and I didn't have to purchase any window coverings. Like playing a tile puzzle, I just rearranged my drapes until the colors and sizes matched the décor. After several tries, I hit upon a combination. I stored the remaining curtains in the basement. They remained there until our next move, when I broke open the box and was surprised anew at what I owned.

"Oh, I forgot I had this cheerful yellow gingham set. And this cabbage rose scarf valance. Isn't it pretty!"

Military wives lead curtain-ready lives. "Custom-made

draperies,"—what's that? Everything I own is fully transportable and meets the international standards for rapid deployment decorating. Although I may have to improvise, it's amazing what I can do with a hot glue gun and staples.

Even when a curtain has outlived its usefulness, I can't let it go. After I got married, my living room valance was a dusty rose plaid. It was a popular color in 1989, but I outgrew it by the next move. Still, I saved the material. While we were living at Fort Leavenworth, Kansas, second-grader Elena burst through the door after school.

"I need a bonnet and an apron for Pioneer Day," she announced.

We plowed through my box of fabric and found the country pink valance.

"This was in our living room when you were a baby," I said, holding it up. "It's perfect for prairie clothes." We fashioned a pattern and sewed the pieces together. Elena placed the bonnet on her head, tied the apron, and twirled in front of the wardrobe mirror.

"Thank you, Mama," she said, skipping out into the fall afternoon.

Watching my little Laura Ingalls Wilder play in the Kansas sun, I realized old curtains never go away. Like the Christmas fruitcake, they just keep turning up some place new.

The Hunt for Hairstylists

This military lifestyle has challenges. Getting reassigned wipes out our checking account. Transporting children and pets across the country makes me grumpy. Acres of unpacked boxes send my blood pressure soaring.

Another seemingly minor concern causes a lot of anxiety—finding a new hairstylist.

The search is difficult because I want a beautician who cuts my hair consistently well, interprets my incoherent ramblings when I ask for a slightly different look, is affordable, and stays in the same place.

My husband has it so easy when it comes to personal grooming. He pulls a number at the exchange barbershop, thumbs through *Esquire* magazine while he waits, then asks for the standard military "high and tight" when it's his turn. After ten minutes, he walks out neatly clipped, tossing a few bills to the cashier.

When I am in a new place and need a haircut, I accost a total stranger who has a style I like and ask her who cut it. Last time, I questioned the waitress at a restaurant where we ate dinner. Her sister, Carrie, was a beautician. I made an appointment with her and was so pleased that I kept going back.

I don't want a "yes woman" for a hairstylist. I pay her to help me look good, so I need honest input.

After several months with Carrie, I plopped down in her chair with my retro-wedge haircut and said, "Same style. Just give me a trim."

"No, I don't think so," she said, shaking her head.

"Excuse me?"

"No, it's too bowly-looking for your face. I want you to grow your bangs out," she said. Rummaging through her comb drawer, she pulled out a picture of a layered bob.

"Like this. And while we're at it," she continued, reclining me back into the shampoo sink, "let's tone down this brassy color."

For three years, I stayed with Carrie. She shared ex-husband horror stories, and I cheered her on as she lost fifty pounds and quit smoking. At Christmas, we exchanged small gifts. Right before I moved, she took me out for lunch.

At other tours, I haven't been as fortunate. For two long years in Georgia, I didn't have the security of that relationship so crucial to my well-being. That was when I discovered that beauticians change salons more often than we move.

The first hairstylist turned out to be from my hometown of Indianapolis. We even knew some of the same people. How lucky!

"I'm sorry. She no longer works here," said the receptionist when I called for a second appointment. "I have no idea where she is."

A friend referred me to another stylist. Before long, she was hired by another shop. She told me beforehand, but didn't volunteer that it was an upscale spa where big tips were encouraged. Fine art and crystal sconces graced the walls. Her station was an antique oak vanity. After our appointment, she handed me a bill in a leather wallet which I was to pay downstairs next to the macrobiotic hair care products.

As much as I liked that "image designer" my budget didn't allow me to follow her. I fled the Persian rugged waiting room. I didn't care if my beautician worked in a strip mall and popped her gum—just give me a decent cut.

The next month, I was so desperate, I dropped into a shop that said "Walk-ins Welcome." Some rookie cut off my bangs practically at the roots. I couldn't look in the mirror for weeks without crying.

I found another stylist in the salon of a large department store. Four weeks later, I called for a trim, but the line was disconnected. The switchboard operator told me the shop had closed. "It was kind of unexpected," she said.

I took a chance and had a beautician in the mall cut my hair. She did a pretty good job for a couple of months. Then I noticed that she had a predominantly older clientele. Instead of youthful and perky, I was morphing into—dare I say it?—matronly. I was too young to look like my mother, so I stopped going there.

Shortly after that, Paul received orders for a PCS move. I would begin my quest in a new town. That is, if I decided to try. A ten-dollar "high and tight" looks mighty appealing.

My Love Affair With Yard Sales

Q: What's the difference between a yard sale and a major
trash pick-up?
A: About twenty feet.

I love yard sales! I put out my junk and others pay cash for it, happy to find it at a cheap price. What a great American institution.

We've averaged two yard sales a year as a military family. Items that are destined for resale get tossed in a big box in the basement. When we've collected enough toys, clothes, shoes, dishes, chair pads, and slipcovers, Paul hauls the booty upstairs. I prowl through closets for any last minute additions.

Not much profit motive goes into pricing. We're just trying to get rid of it. I slap adhesive sales tags on the inventory, change a twenty dollar bill for ones, brew the thermal carafe of coffee, and open for business. At the end of the day, we have some petty cash.

Military families live leanly. Like snakes, we shed our skins every season. We don't want to drag excess baggage to another set of dinky quarters. It's better to travel light.

Or so I thought. Every time we move, I'm amazed how much junk we've accumulated. It's all because of impulse buying and a lot of great ideas that never panned out.

"What were these for?" said Paul, holding up a sealed package of bed sheets printed with sailboats.

"I was going to make a valance and shower curtain for our nautical themed bathroom," I said.

"What nautical themed bathroom?" he said. Exactly.

"How about that?" he said, pointing to a green sundress with price tags still attached.

"It was on clearance, and I couldn't resist," I said. "I figured I'd lose weight and it would fit."

He wisely didn't pursue the subject.

If yard sales are a great institution, then "The Great American Yard Sale" at Fort Leavenworth, Kansas, was the Olympics, the World Cup, and Daytona Bike Week rolled into one. The post announced the date in the spring, issued guidelines, and installed portable toilets at strategic locations. Little did we know what to expect.

According to the rules, buying was to begin at 8 a.m. By 5:30, the headlights and engine noise on the road outside woke me up.

"People are here already," Paul said. "Let's get our table out." Since we had purged our belongings only ten months earlier, our offerings were meager. Nevertheless, eager customers snapped them up.

Soon the traffic was bumper-to-bumper. Swells of people from Kansas and Missouri descended on "The Fort," as they called it, for the highest concentration of bargains known to mankind.

The rookies showed up with no way to transport their loot, not even a shopping bag. Professional grade shoppers had trained for this day. They rigged up sophisticated load-bearing equipment. One woman, who bought my baby toys, rolled an elaborate contraption of milk crates lashed together with bungee cords.

Some brought their children's wagons outfitted with makeshift racks. A man dragged a huge wheeled trash bin. I saw several garden carts and jogging strollers pressed into service.

By 9 a.m., business tapered off, and I had to leave for my computer class at the community college. Paul minded the store while I inched out of the cul-de-sac. Throngs of people circulated through the housing area. It looked like Fifth Avenue at Christmas. Cars lined both shoulders on the road. The field outside the main gate was crowded with semi-trucks and RVs. I saw a gentleman, clearly a swap meet dealer, zip by in a golf cart, unload inventory, and head back into the maelstrom.

When I returned at noon, the place looked like the locusts had swarmed.

"We made almost a hundred dollars," Paul announced.

I cruised the street for last minute mark-downs. I found a pair of rain boots in my size for two dollars. Then I saw a German Potato cart marked "$100."

"How about forty dollars?" I asked.

"Fifty," he countered.

"I'll take it."

Net yard sale profits were $48, and I was only two blocks from my house. I turned around before I spent our entire windfall.

On the way home, I bought a baseball glove for Stephen and a lens for my camera.

Chickpea and Okra Quiche

About two weeks before a move, I stop going to the commissary except to buy milk. I have a permanent-change-of-station mission ahead of me: to combine the remaining groceries into meals before we depart.

Most military wives I know excel at this same challenge. I practice it every month—the last few dinners before payday when I have no money in the checking account to buy groceries. I have to feed my family *something* so I concoct a semi-nutritious (or at least filling) meal out of the scraps in my cupboard. I am terribly creative at it, with "terribly" being the operative word here—a can of corn, a bag of split peas, some bacon bits, and *Voila!* a hearty soup!

At moving time, the stakes are higher. It's a game of Culinary Scrabble. The object is to work my way through the fridge and the pantry. The prize for an empty cupboard? A dinner containing all four food groups at a local restaurant.

In my house, the first few dinners under the PCS Rations Reduction Act resemble normal meals except for one quirky addition. I'll serve ravioli with a side dish of cranberry sauce, for example. The cranberries have been in the freezer since Thanksgiving. It's now May.

If I study the odds and ends in the kitchen long enough, a menu gradually takes shape. From the freezer, for example, I produce an icy package of carbon-dated pork chops. When thawed, I top them with a can of cream of, let's call it "question mark soup," (the label was removed for a school fund raiser), bake at 350 for an hour, and serve it with salsa and those withered oranges at the back of the produce drawer. Done!

For an entrée the next day, I simmer dried lima beans with the bonus ham hock that I was delighted to find frozen to yesterday's pork chops. Instant mashed potatoes and cottage cheese round out the scrumptious meal. I think, "This is going really well!"

The following night my family pleads for take-out pizza, but I refuse, gesturing with delight at one bare refrigerator shelf. Besides, the biscuits, bologna, and carrot stick dinner is almost ready.

The next evening, my husband suggests we go out. "No way!" I argue. "We still have lots of food."

"Honey," he begs hungrily, "steak sauce is not a main dish." Imagine his surprise when I present him with my latest concoction: chickpea and okra quiche.

The challenge continues to its unappetizing low point about three days before the move. In the midst of chaotic relocation preparations, I pile cookbooks around me, looking for a recipe that calls for chicken bouillon, mandarin oranges, brown sugar, jalapenos, marshmallows, vanilla pudding, and some mysterious leftover which I later discover to be Play-doh.

My husband and children, who by now are considering a crisis intervention for me, begin setting out on mysterious afternoon errands. More than once I've found concealed McDonald's bags under the car seat. They'll eat the swill from the local burger joint, but turn their noses up at my culinary innovations. I just don't get it.

My crackpot spin on the domestic arts has become an obsession. Each empty container I throw in the recycling bin fills me with smugness. When I wipe down my bare refrigerator, I'm a proud woman. (In the interest of public safety, I do throw away whatever unidentified masses remain.) Then I arrange the molasses, confectioner's sugar, lasagna noodles, and vegetable oil on a tray and present it to a deserving neighbor.

About this time, I notice the school lunch menu printed in the newspaper. For the last week of school, it just reads, "Springtime Surprise." Even the cafeteria ladies go through a summer clean out. I like their terminology so much, I'm adopting it for our next move. "Springtime Surprise": it's what's for dinner!

A Sports Fan Without a Team

I was an Air Force brat. After college, I served in the Army for five years. Now I am the wife of an active duty soldier. It recently dawned on me that after a lifetime of moving around with the military, I missed out on something important to the average American: I have no devotion to a professional sports team.

By devotion, I mean the mania possessed by fans who regularly wear clothing with franchise emblems. Those supporters that can tell you why the head coach should be fired, who must lose in order to make the play-offs, or how they've never in their history "clinched it" this early. Passionate fans can recap any match-up from the last decade. They live for home games; a win or loss dictates their mood for a week.

How thrilling to have an obsession so powerful! I'd gladly paint letters on my body for that moment of glory on national television. Or shell out a week's pay for a ticket to "the big game." Such unconditional loyalty is missing in my life.

Some people are rabid about college sports. For example, many Arkansas Razorback fans travel in RVs to every football game. I heard that one couple even missed their daughter's wedding. (They made it to the reception however.) Okay, that is a bit much, but you've got to admire their zeal.

During graduate school at Florida State University, Paul and I were Seminole fans. We wore garnet and gold and went to all the home football games. We tailgated alongside the motor homes. The 'Noles won the national championship that year. It was a heady time.

When we moved two years later, the Seminoles became like the West Point team Paul cheers for, and my alma mater, William and Mary. We hold them with warm affection and wish them the best, but we don't participate with gusty in the Gators rivalry anymore. All I can claim now is a lukewarm geographical affinity with the nearest professional team. I pledge my undying allegiance, as long as we share the same local calling area. When we lived in northern Virginia I followed the Redskins and the Orioles. At Fort Leavenworth we cheered the Kansas City Royals and the Chiefs. Fort Campbell made me a Tennessee Titans fan. I dated but didn't get serious.

At my age, 43, I may be too old to make a real commitment. One gets hard-wired for the home team early. A newcomer is always open to accusations of Johnny-come-lately-ism, and rightly so. I've got no pedigree.

I worried that my son Stephen would suffer the same fate. Being a nomadic Army kid, would he have the chance to love and honor a team forever and ever? He flirted with the Yankees when he was a three-year old in New York, but his affection didn't survive the move to the Midwest. Stephen was eight when we relocated to Rhode Island in 2002, and he had a life-changing event: he became a Red Sox fan.

"Why did you let him do that?" my Brooklyn uncle scolded me. "You've just set him up for a lifetime of disappointment."

But it was out of my control. Stephen was mesmerized by the intense baseball culture in the Northeast. It was the perfect convergence of his boyish exuberance, the region, and the vibe all happening at a time when his love for the sport blossomed. He owns ten Red Sox t-shirts and one lovingly shaped, sweat-streaked hat. Ask him his favorite destination and he'll say, "Fenway Park."

In Stephen's second year of Boston loyalty, the Sox did the impossible and won the World Series. That settled it for him. This was no superficial crush. The Red Sox had mutated his DNA. Wherever the Army sends us, Stephen will check the local listings for games, even invest in satellite TV if necessary. It's part of his identity now. Stephen has the brass ring; I have the sports void.

"Cheer up, honey," said Paul, himself a wanderer in the pro league wilderness. "We still have the Army-Navy game."

Scenes from that heroic clash flashed before my eyes. I saw ships burned in effigy, fighter fly-bys, parachute drops, presidential appearances, cadets and midshipmen playing their hearts out.

That will have to do.

It's a good substitute.

Resource Reallocation Specialist

I'm excited about a decorating trend called "Shabby Chic." Designers claim they just invented this faded, gently used look. I've embraced it for years.

As newlyweds with one income and a baby on the way, Paul and I had no money to purchase new furniture. What we didn't get as hand-me-downs we bought at flea markets or yard sales. Another way we acquired possessions was by dumpster diving. Having poked through roadside trash for years, I have elevated it to an art form.

I'd rather not be called a dumpster diver, looter, scavenger, or any other unseemly name I've heard whispered behind my back. I prefer instead the title of "Resource Reallocation Specialist." I'm proud to serve as a secondary market for unwanted items.

Walking for exercise is a great way to scout out garbage. I route my early morning walks through upscale neighborhoods on trash day. The smaller collectibles—the picture frames and children's toys—I take with me right then. I return later with the car for bigger items. This is how I got my file cabinet and my office chair. One morning I passed a friend who was reallocating a perfectly good dresser into her minivan. And need I mention what happens in late spring when one third of the people on base purge their household goods in preparation for a move? Every rubbish pile becomes a reallocation specialist's paradise.

My husband used to be mortified at my lowbrow habit. Now he abets with equal enthusiasm. His change of heart came when we found a box of hardback books on the curb. It was the mother lode of military history—*At Dawn We Slept, Campaigns of Napoleon,* and *Eisenhower's Lieutenants,* to name a few. All were in good condition, some were still wrapped in cellophane. Paul now boasts that half of his professional library came from roadside refuse.

These days a pile of stacked trash catches his eye. Occasionally, he'll come home from a jog with a coil of nylon rope, a length of fencing, or some 4x4's he needed for a project—all retrieved from the curb. His plunder included a perfectly good molded plastic doghouse, which we later sold at a yard sale for thirty dollars. I'm so proud of my apprentice.

By order of a Supreme Court ruling, resource reallocation is not considered theft or trespassing. Garbage is public domain. Still, while it's legal, some people—my daughter is one of them—would argue that resource reallocation is an unbecoming habit. One day while driving home, my husband and I saw an electric patio grill with a sign on it that said, "Free." Paul slammed on the brakes. Much to my pre-teen's horror, we began loading the grill into the back of the SUV. Elena ducked beneath the seats so no one would recognize her.

"Really, Mom," she wailed from the floorboards, "You're taking this 'one man's trash is another man's treasure' way too seriously!"

"It's free!" I replied happily. As the goddess of junk, I've always said it's amazing what you can find if you have no self-respect. In the name of Resource Reallocation, I've waded into construction dumpsters and picked through my neighbor's cast-offs in broad daylight.

"I'm never going out with you people again!" Elena screamed. "*Never!*" Paul laughed. We were in marvelous moods because we needed a new grill. A quick clean-up with a wire brush and we'd be cooking steak that night.

Rookies in the Real Estate Market

After ten years of living in government quarters or rentals, we took a leap and bought a house in Clarksville, Tennessee. It was a beautiful two-story, red brick Georgian home on a large lot with trees.

At the closing the title officer slid a towering stack of paperwork across the table. "Sign at all the red tabs," he instructed.

The total dollar amount had a few more digits than I was prepared for.

"Wow, are we really responsible for that much?"

"It's better not to look," our agent said.

I couldn't speak for a week.

By the eighth day I was sitting up and taking clear liquids. Doctors predicted a full recovery.

I was still fragile from my trauma when a new neighbor stopped by.

"You must be staying in Clarksville," she said. "You own a house."

"Not exactly," I said. "We're just paying high rent. It's called a mortgage."

Paul and I ignored the conventional wisdom that you have to own a house for five years to break even. Even though our tour at Fort Campbell would be three years at the most, I was tired of the cramped living on post and longed for a backyard with privacy. I wanted to plant perennials and paint rooms, so we took a financial loss in exchange for a higher quality of life.

For the length of our tour, it was great. We had a garage! We had a deck! We had a bay window in the kitchen! We had an ice maker in our freezer! We had arrived!

Then it was time to sell.

"I don't think we'll have a problem finding a buyer. Look at this view," I said, sweeping my arms towards the lush wood line in the backyard.

"At this price range, it takes a while," our Realtor clucked. "The housing market is kind of flat right now." Her voice trailed off.

We ceremoniously planted a "For Sale" in the front yard and waited for the buyers to beat down our door.

And they did pop in all the time, usually with five minute's notice, to find me frantically making beds and clearing breakfast dishes. A steady stream of prospective homeowners traipsed through, but nobody made an offer. Our agent asked for feedback from her colleagues.

"They didn't like the paint scheme."

"The backyard was too big."

"They wanted a bedroom on the first floor."

"The husband worried about drainage on the lot."

Two other houses in our neighborhood with identical floor plans went on the market. One was built on a steep slope and had a retaining wall to keep the yard from sliding into the street. The other was set in a low-lying ditch.

They both sold.

"But why?" I wailed to our agent. "Our house has a nicer lot and it's on a cul-de-sac!"

"Let's reduce the price," she said.

"I hope this works," Paul said. "It has to sell before we leave."

The "REDUCED" banner went on the sign. We became "motivated sellers." I chewed my nails.

Another month passed. Well-meaning friends inundated me with their horror stories.

"We had double house payments for four months," said Linda. "We went through our savings."

"Our house was empty for nine months!" countered Amy.

My sister reminded me that she had to come up with fifteen thousand dollars at the closing to unload her house.

I started twitching. Words began catching in my throat.

Would this beautiful house lead us to bankruptcy?

Elena and I drove to the religious icon store and bought a statue of Saint Joseph, the patron saint of real estate. We buried it in the flower bed as the instructions said. Just for good measure, I sprinkled fairy dust, scattered four leaf clovers, and left a rabbit's foot.

After three weeks of prayer and meditation, still nothing.

"Let's reduce it again," said our agent.

"We'll lose money," Paul said.

"Maybe," she replied, "but if it sits empty, you'll lose a lot more." I began to wonder about her stake in this.

"I think it's time to consider renting," I said. Being an absentee landlord didn't thrill me, but I wanted to cut our losses. The moving date was fast approaching.

Within days of listing it in the classifieds, we had a tenant and I breathed easily again.

I explained to our agent that her services were no longer needed.

"So you found someone to pay the big bucks you wanted?" she asked snidely.

We rented to the same family for two years. When they announced they were moving to another city, Paul and I decided to try selling again. This time, we chose a different real estate agent.

I bit the bullet and prepared to eat a couple of mortgage payments.

The first day that the house was open for showing a couple toured it. Two days later they made an offer. We countered, they accepted, and we set a closing date.

"It was those woods in the backyard," our Realtor explained. "The wife loved the view from the bay window."

"Let's Be Tourists!"

That was my comment to Paul as I spread out the newspaper on the table after breakfast. On Thursdays, the *Journal* carried all the happenings for the upcoming weekend. I began circling items with my highlighter.

Technically, we weren't tourists in Rhode Island; we were residents. We received an electric bill with our name and address printed on it. We had library cards, but since we'd only just moved here, I was eager to start exploring.

As social director of the family, I mobilized a cast of complaining characters to tour wonders in the local area. This conflicted with their natural inclinations. Paul wanted to putter around the house. Elena and Stephen would rather stick toothpicks under their fingernails than endure the company of parents. Nevertheless, using threats and blackmail, I coerced them into the car.

"Here's the plan," I said. "Farmers' market, Chowder Cook-off, mansion tour."

"Boring."

"Gross."

"Yuck."

"Cheer up," I said, fastening my seatbelt. "It could be an art museum."

"Double yuck," Paul replied.

"If you're good we'll skip the mansion."

As a military family, we have to keep in mind our finite stay at each duty station. I became the minister of family fun because I knew what would happen with a "get around to it someday" approach. We'd never actually do anything before the next orders arrived. Our timelines weren't open-ended, so we had to appreciate our surroundings from the beginning.

I learned this lesson in my younger days. When I was an

undergraduate at William and Mary College, I rarely visited Colonial Williamsburg, which was free with my student ID. Now I pay the going rate to tour, just like the throngs of Americans who make a special trip to see it. I had unconsciously adopted a local's attitude—townies never went to the Governor's Mansion or the Blacksmith Shop. Williamsburg was just a scenic backdrop to them.

Looking at it through my rearview mirror after graduation, I vowed never to make that mistake again. Today, instead of backwards glances filled with regret, I marvel at the sights through the windshield as we arrive.

I call this the "Brownie Perspective." My son and I once took a three-day trip to New York City. We told a friend about *The Lion King* on Broadway, the Empire State Building, and our harbor cruise.

"You've now seen more of the city than I have," said Karen, "and I grew up on Long Island. Thank goodness for my Brownie Troop, or I never would have seen the Statue of Liberty."

So, we're Brownies. We're excited. We take field trips.

"How do you find out about all this stuff?" my neighbor asked as we returned from a Saturday Fishing Derby.

"She can't pass a brochure rack without grabbing half of them," Paul muttered.

"Or a bulletin board," Stephen chimed in.

I pored over listings in the paper, devoured Welcome Packets, scribbled notes on the calendar—"Daffodil Festival," "Honeybee Demonstration."

Nothing was too small or unimportant to note. Even in remote areas I soaked up the local color: the Boll Weevil monument in Alabama, small town rodeos, the Peanut Festival. (It was worth it just to see the young woman crowned "Peanut Queen.")

My children were rarely joyful participants. They'd rather pass on the visit to the Pony Express Museum/Oregon

Trail/Museum of Country Music/Washington Monument/Mount Vernon/Mammoth Cave/Plymouth Rock. It didn't matter where we lived in America. The answer was "No."

While in New England we took them to Lexington and Concord in Massachusetts. I was mesmerized by Walden Pond. Paul rhapsodized about the Revolutionary War. Elena and Stephen had one response:

"Can we go back to the hotel pool now?"

Ah, but they won't remember swimming at the Holiday Inn Express. As the negative associations fade, they'll appreciate the stimulating experiences we force fed them through the years.

Speaking of feeding, after thoughtfully sipping two-ounce chowder samples from every restaurant on the Eastern Seaboard, the four of us waddled off the Newport Pier, holding our sloshing and bloated bellies. We had consumed four bowls of soup each.

"Mom," said Elena.

I turned, expecting a warm "Thank You" for orchestrating another delightful slice of Americana.

"If I ever see clam chowder again," she warned, "I'm gonna spew."

Grandmother's Piano

During a recent fundraiser at the Country Music Hall of Fame and Museum, singer Vince Gill played a guitar owned by the late Johnny Cash. While reading about it in our local newspaper, I was surprised that the guitar wasn't safely stored in a display case.

"The biggest disservice you can do to an instrument is to lock it away," the article quoted Gill. "They never get played and they lose their soul."

I understood completely. My grandmother's piano is in our living room, although I don't play. After a few semesters of unsuccessful lessons in college I gave up.

"I had a musical by-pass when I was very young," I explained to the teacher. Hard to believe I descended from Elizabeth Ashburn, a talented pianist and organist. Music was how she expressed her soul. She taught lessons and played at church. Although she died in 1991, we have her spirit with us in this elegant Sohmer console.

After Grandma downsized to an apartment at a retirement community, her piano, gathering dust in my Dad's living room, was used only to display photographs and plants. Occasionally, when I was home, I banged out the only song I knew—"Amazing Grace"—but the keys were so out of tune it was agonizing, even by my standards. Grandma's piano was losing its soul.

Several years later, I married Paul and we had our daughter Elena. My dad agreed to give me the piano. We rented a trailer and transported it from Indianapolis to our apartment in Florida.

That was five moves ago. Carting a piano in and out of semi-trucks has been hard on it. There's a gash in the leg deep enough to rest my pinkie. I caress the disfigured wood as if it were a wound. "I'm so sorry," I whisper.

The movers made no secret of how much they disliked it.

"Looky there," shouted the wiry crew leader with the big attitude as he opened the van in Kansas. "They've got a 'pee-nano.'" He impatiently tried to wrestle it away from the door. Finally, five strong guys lifted the heavy instrument onto the ramp.

"Let's just roll it down," one said, pointing to the quarter-sized wheels which were intended only to scoot it around the parlor. "Somebody catch it at the bottom."

I lunged forward to keep my piano from being splintered into the curb.

"Go somewhere else," Paul grabbed me. "I'll take care of this."

I went inside to make space for it. The crew, lugging with micro-movements under Paul's watchful eye, rolled the piano into the living room. Then, amazingly, one of the movers asked if he might play for a moment.

"Go ahead," I said. "It's a little out of tune."

Amid the chaos of boxes he mesmerized us with a mood-softening sonata.

"That was nice," I said. "How long have you been taking lessons?"

"I've just kind of, you know, been playing all my life." He returned to the keys. I saw that his posture was not music-school stiff, nor his fingers curved and pressing like levers as I had learned. Probably self-taught, I decided, but obviously a natural. Head gently swaying, he coaxed music from the ivories like a virtuoso.

Grandma would've been pleased.

I'm happy to see her talent emerge in Elena. A tall, beautiful, sensitive girl, she began lessons in second grade. After a move and a series of instructors she didn't click with, she announced, "I quit. I'm no good at music."

"She's only on sabbatical," I told Paul when he objected. "Give her time."

Sure enough, two years later, she started tentatively tickling the ivories again. "Don't listen!" she yelled, when I peeked around the corner. So I stood in the kitchen and eavesdropped.

"Our piano player's back," I thought. Now, every evening as she practices, we are awash with rondos, andantes, and minuets. The air in the house swells with her trills and grace notes. I'll never forget at her birthday party how the girls gathered around Elena at the piano and belted out "My Heart Will Go On" from *Titanic*.

There may be scratches on the leg and cracks in the encasement, but Elena has put the soul back into Grandma's piano.

Reinventing the Holidays

Last March, my friend Sue asked me what we were doing for Easter.

"We're staying here," I said, meaning Rhode Island, where my husband worked in the ROTC Department at the local university. "Maybe boil some seafood for dinner. You know, the traditional Easter lobster," I smiled.

Inside, I cringed. I hated confessing that we had no holiday plans. I assumed everyone was attending large family gatherings. We had no kin within an easy drive, and no friends or neighbors had thought to include us, the lone Army family, in their day. The big "L" for loser burned my forehead.

"I love to hear what you do for the holidays," said Sue. "It's always different. We do the same thing every year. We get together with family."

My jaw dropped. I was ashamed because we were stuck at home without family. Why in the world would she envy me?

"It would be nice to go somewhere by ourselves for once," she mused, "but there would be hurt feelings." All her holidays were spoken for. There were pumpkin carvings in the fall, lamb at her mother's for Easter, and summers at the lake with cousins.

How could the conventional trappings of Christmas and Easter be a burden? My sense of isolation lifted ever so slightly. Maybe "creative control" of our holidays was an advantage I hadn't considered. Traditional celebrations were problematic for military folks. Going "over the river and through the woods" involved great distances and hundreds of dollars. Since we had little children, our road show included car seats, strollers, cribs, diaper bags, toys, and over-tired preschoolers. It was a recipe for disaster.

My neighbor on post once told me how they drove from New York to Michigan to Florida and back between Christmas and New Year's.

"We wanted to see both parents," she said. "We ended up exhausted and our families were mad at us for not staying longer. It was the last time we did that."

Our friends, Matt and Ellen, always spend the holiday at their house, wherever they're stationed. If they travel, they do it after December 25. During our three assignments together, we often saw them drag their tree out to the curb on the 26th before visiting family in Ohio. But Christmas morning, eve, and dinner were in their own nest.

"The grandparents realize it's nothing personal," Ellen said. "We have our own traditions."

Once I escaped the conventional structure of How Things Should Be, I felt liberated. Our holidays had been unique and memorable. One year in Washington D.C., we had Thanksgiving Dinner at the Fort Myer dining facility. We filed through the cafeteria line as cooks heaped turkey and fixings on our trays. That there was no china, linen, or sterling didn't matter. The place had its own charm.

In 2001 at Fort Campbell, Paul had just returned from Kosovo, and the kids couldn't get enough of him. On Christmas Day, I watched them snuggle together on the couch, all still in pajamas. A free day awaited us. I padded into the kitchen for more coffee. Biscuit, our black lab, followed me, pressing his cold nose into my hand.

"Hey," I said, poking my head back in the living room. "Anyone for a walk?" Once dressed, we drove to a nearby park and hiked in the hushed woods, Biscuit loping happily alongside.

Later that afternoon we visited our friends, the Hollands, for an old-fashioned pitch-in. An apple pie, warm from the oven, rested in my lap. Elena carried the poinsettia and the porcelain ornaments we had wrapped as gifts. When we arrived, Marty was carving the Christmas ham and Anne was pouring drinks. Before long Robin and Glenn showed up with their two daughters.

Perfect.

Holidays mean finding rest, renewal, and delight, wherever we are, whomever we're with. Before I tear into my Easter lobster, I'll deliver this toast in Sue's honor: "To traditions, new and old."

Marriage

If marriage is only for the strong, then a military marriage is only for the Herculean. With the Global War on Terror, active duty personnel can deploy one out of every three years. Even when units are not overseas, extended train-ups and long duty days are normal. Despite the pressures of absence and readjustment, the commitment persists.

Love is a Battlefield

As newlyweds, my husband and I visited Amelia Island, Florida, for some sun and relaxation. Paul, an infantry officer, wanted to see Fort Clinch, a pre-Civil War garrison. We stopped by for what I thought would be a quick visit before a romantic beach picnic. My groom, however, had other ideas. We stayed there for most of the morning. I tapped my foot and rolled my eyes while he inspected every inch of the fort with boyish delight and absorption. The cannons, ramparts, and bunkers captured more of his attention than I did. When I threatened a tantrum to rival any Civil War battle, we reluctantly departed.

That was my introduction to Paul's obsession with all American military history sites. His idea of a really fun weekend was battlefield hopping. I was a hostile witness. At Gettysburg National Park I fell asleep during the introductory lecture in the visitor's center. I don't even think Paul heard me snoring.

"Wasn't that great!" he raved. "That light board was amazing! I understand things I never did before!" He was glowing. I mentioned leaving; I was pregnant, tired, and hungry. Ignoring my complaints, Paul and his fellow lieutenant loaded me in the car for a three-hour, stop-and-start crawl through the park's major points of interest.

"Pickett's Charge. Great," I muttered from the back seat.

To me, American history was boring. Wars and treaties, that's all it was. I discouraged Paul's habit of visiting battle sites. If I spotted a brown state park sign along the highway, I diverted his attention until we were safely past it. Unfortunately, since we lived in Virginia at the time, historic markers popped up like state troopers on a holiday weekend. My finest escape-and-evade procedures were often unsuccessful.

Innocent recreational excursions often ended at historic sites. A shortcut to avoid I-95 traffic led us right to a shrine to

Stonewall Jackson. On our way to pick strawberries, we stumbled on Wilderness Battlefield. The route to a new mall went, coincidentally, right by Spotsylvania Courthouse.

"Well, as long as we're here," Paul said, turning the car into the parking lot.

During a trip from Indiana to Florida, stormy weather forced us to stop for the night at a motel in Tennessee.

"What do you know?" Paul said, as he surveyed the map after dinner. "Shiloh Battlefield is right down the road."

I resigned myself to accompanying him occasionally. That would be our sole diversion if it were up to him, so I rationed them. Then I discovered many of these "A List" historic attractions were situated next to charming towns featuring antique stores, boutiques, and ferny cafés with stone fireplaces. From then on, battle sites included retail therapy and a cozy bistro lunch.

Under our agreeable arrangement trips to Harper's Ferry and Manassas quickly followed. Despite my best attempts to stay apathetic, I became interested in the Civil War. I had always imagined that Northern and Southern Armies fought in hollers and clearings no bigger than, say, the Piggly-Wiggly parking lot. The truth was that generals commanded conflicts spanning a county without so much as a walkie-talkie. Anyone who has chaperoned a preschool trip to the petting zoo can appreciate the logistics of this feat.

Like the man who gave his wife a drill press for Christmas, I bought Paul a coffee table book on the Civil War. This was the *People* magazine of references—glossy pages with full-color photographs and lively text. By the time we visited Antietam I was consulting my, uh, *his* Civil War book regularly. I lugged it up the observation platform so I could compare the view with the one in the book.

When we watched the Ken Burns television series on the Civil War, I recognized many landscapes we had visited. Even three-year old Elena pointed at the cannons on the television.

"We went there!" she shouted.

As I listened to the journal entries and letters in the documentary, I realized that history was much more than wars and treaties. With first-person narrative, it became, like literature, a good story. I could relate to this as an English major. While Paul still focused on the strategies and blunders of the war, I savored the unremarkable glimpses into the hearts of the soldiers and their families. History became human.

Brown state park signs used to provoke a fight-or-flight response in me. Now I look forward to each impromptu stop. While stationed in Virginia we exhausted all the Civil War sites. Now we live in New England where there is a fresh complement of Revolutionary War points of interest. There are also plenty of literary places, a point I bring up with alarming regularity. This Saturday we are going to Massachusetts for the annual re-enactment of the Battle of Lexington. But on Sunday we'll be in Concord, touring the homes of Thoreau, Emerson, and Louisa May Alcott.

Field Time and Temporary Duty

After a demanding year in command, neighbor Nancy's husband took three weeks of leave to spend some "quality time" with the family. After the first week he started to get on Nancy's nerves. He counseled her on more space efficient ways to load the dishwasher. At the commissary he pointed out that the brands she bought were not the most economical. Furthermore, the snacks she gave the boys contained entirely too much sugar.

"You're driving me crazy!" Nancy exploded. "This is a frightening snapshot of our retirement."

For all the complaints about temporary duty and field time in military life, they can be a blessing. In moderation, they provide the short but welcome respites from one another that are essential for an enduring marriage. One battalion commander promised his troops no field time for three months after they returned from Operation Just Cause. After a month, two desperate wives cornered the commander's wife at the commissary.

"You've got to get your husband to send these guys out to the field," they begged her.

"You're telling me," she said, looking just as ragged.

Time apart from each other is like the pause in a musical composition—it enhances the whole. While my military man is away all schedules are moot. There is popcorn for supper, or maybe lunch at the local food court. After the children are tucked in bed, a long, luxurious evening stretches before me. I dig out those scrapbook projects, or curl up in front of a chick flick.

For the first three days I delight in the precious privacy. Then a curious thing happens. I start to miss him. My collection of resentments is replaced with soft-focus happily-ever-aftering. His good qualities come out in relief. All the reasons I fell in love with him trickle back into my consciousness. Not only that, but I feel recharged. The relaxed demands on my time freed me to do some self-pampering, whether it's catching up on correspondence or reading a Sidney Sheldon novel. I'm in a much better mood.

I unexpectedly found out that my husband agreed with this philosophy. As he was packing to leave for a field exercise I teased him, "You're going to miss me while you're gone, aren't you?"

"Of course," he said. He walked down the hall and I heard him mumble, "After the first couple days."

Finding a balance is the key. Taking a break from each other every now and then is good. In military life there's the danger that absences can be too long or frequent—often with damaging consequences. But let's talk about the effort of too much togetherness. When my husband started a job as a staff officer I asked, "How often will you have to go to the field?"

"Never."

"How about TDY?"

"None."

No TDY. No field time. It's going to be a long year.

Purchased in Your Absence

I think the minister secretly inserted the phrase, "You may now start complaining about what your wife buys" into our wedding vows. From the moment we became a couple, Paul has lectured me about finances.

"I have to buy things for our home," I said. He had no appreciation for décor. If it were up to him, we'd be sitting in canvas director's chairs and stacking our CDs on cinderblock shelves. We would, however, have a kick-butt stereo system with speakers the size of Stonehenge. Rather than debate each "frivolous" purchase I resorted to a different tactic.

I began to make all my major purchases while Paul was gone. Since he was in the Army, he was deployed or on temporary duty a lot. His absences came in handy while I accessorized our quarters. My friend Susan taught me that it was easier to seek forgiveness than receive permission. Whenever her husband went out of town, she bought Oriental rugs. Judging by the fact that every room had one, he was gone a lot.

Susan lived in a town crowded with factory outlets, and she invited me to visit her while Paul was away. I was solo parenting a newborn and ready for some "retail therapy."

On the first day of shopping, I found my china pattern in a discount shop. I thought the serving platter, coffee pot, sugar bowl, and creamer would be a great addition to my set. There was the tiny problem of how much all that bone china cost—over $200. But what a great price for a completer set!

"Buy it," Susan whispered in my ear like Satan's little helper.

"Paul will blow a gasket if I spend that much money," I said.

"Paul Schmall! He's gone for three more weeks. File the credit card bill before he gets home," she said. "He'll never know."

I bought the china. Months later Paul asked me where we got the serving platter.

"I can't remember exactly," I said. "I think it was a wedding present."

It was a gift all right, the gift of subterfuge. If I waited until he left, I could buy anything without cross examination.

Sometimes I tried to make it seem like Paul was in the decision loop, but that was just a formality. While he took a group of colleagues to study Gettysburg National Battlefield, I drove to northern Virginia to visit our friends Brad and Erin. I found out they were trying to sell their SUV. We were looking for a second car, and theirs met our criteria. Best of all, the price was right. I called around for a good interest rate. The credit union faxed me paper work, and I had the car appraised.

Then I drove it to Gettysburg, where Paul was doing "important research." With my soft-shoe approach, I wanted him to think that buying the car was a great move. I talked market value, four doors, mileage, and stereo. He took it for a test drive.

"It's a manly car," I hinted.

"Let's call the bank tomorrow. See what they say," was his final delay tactic.

I smiled brightly and produced the folder of loan forms. "Got all that information right here," I said. "Check out that low rate." I tapped the papers with my pen. "Just need your signature." It was best to present him with a done deal. Otherwise things got tied up in committee.

"Why are you grinning like that?" he said. Reluctantly, he signed and drove the car home. His Gettysburg excursion cost him $13,000 and he was only gone four days. I used to rail against Paul's absences. It wasn't pretty, but that armoire, those sconces, that painting, and our 400 thread count sheets are sure pretty.

Confessions of a Complaining Military Wife

A commander once ran into one of his soldiers and asked, "How's your wife?"

"Complaining, but not mutinous, sir," he answered.

I confess that in 16 years of marriage, I've been a marathon complainer.

I've asked my husband many times to get out of the Army.

I've cursed this military life through clenched teeth. I've yelled, begged, and cried.

I've invoked the name of my college roommate, Marsha, who married an investment banker and planned to move into her third home, a custom design, just as soon as they returned from their Caribbean vacation. Meanwhile, we were living in a duplex on post with a carport and cinderblock walls. *Cinderblock.* At least this time they were painted.

"When am I going to get a decent house to live in?" I yelled. Or, "When is *my* life going to start?" I usually emphasized these rhetorical questions by slamming my fist on the nearest table.

During my rants Paul acted like he might consider resigning from the Army and taking a job with more pay and stability. At the very least he might begin a dialogue about it. But then he went on doing exactly what he'd been doing, and I fumed.

Obviously, being married to a man in the military hasn't been all sweetness and light. I am not a service wife who chirps, "I have always supported him 100%. His career is our number one priority."

No, at the low points, I've threatened to walk out. I've circled rental home ads in the classifieds and announced, "We'll be here. Visit when you can." In the end, however, I moved with him. Not cheerfully, mind you, but I did.

When I mentioned my struggles to a college friend, who also

married a serviceman, she admitted feeling the same way. "I even knew what I was getting myself into," she said, referring to her upbringing as an Army brat.

We both knew marriages that fractured over the pressures imposed by the lifestyle. Witnessing friends divorce stimulated a lot of uncomfortable conversations.

"Well, *she* just wasn't happy. *She* had problems," Paul said.

"This isn't an easy life for a woman," I replied. "It's not fun leaving your friends every few years."

Prior to one divorce, the husband went to Korea for an unaccompanied tour while his wife and their three children moved to her hometown in Florida. When he returned after a year, she told him they were not following him to his next assignment in Kansas. She had a good job, the children were doing well in school, and the family was happily settled in their new house. The marriage ended. He continued with his Army career.

"How could she do that to her family?" my shocked husband asked.

"Maybe she thought that stability and predictability, not to mention a more satisfied mother, *was* the best thing for her family," I said. "Did you ever think about that?" I followed him from room to room. "Maybe, just maybe, bouncing around the country wasn't her idea of a great life."

Paul must have noted my manic eyes and the perspiration on my upper lip. He glanced towards the door, and did the only thing an infantryman could do—he escaped and evaded.

After my hostility subsided, Paul tentatively stuck his head in the living room.

"Armed truce?" he suggested.

"It's not fair," I said. "All those anniversaries alone."

Paul listened.

"That awful summer in temporary quarters."

He looked like he might consider resigning from the Army.

"The wonderful job I had to quit because we moved." At the very least he might begin a dialogue about it. He stared at me.

"How are you really?" he finally asked.

"Complaining, but not mutinous," I said.

He went back to what he'd been doing.

Stack Containment

I organize by stacks. That's the method that works best for me, but it drives my husband crazy. Paul calls them my "Little Sarajevos" and avoids them like toxic waste.

"Make files!" he counsels me.

"Files, piles, whatever," I say. "That's just geography. I like to leave things out so I can fiddle with them."

"How do you find anything?" he asks, as I rifle through papers.

"I know which quadrant of the house it's in. If it's in the bottom right, it's either by the phone, on the stairs, or on top of the buffet."

In all areas except his sock drawer, Paul is meticulous. He makes choices and acts promptly. Desks are cleared and in-boxes emptied at the end of each day. But Paul doesn't screen the tidal wave of catalogs, school announcements, team rosters, lunch menus, newsletters, and permission slips that comes through our door everyday. Half of it goes directly in the recycling bin. Still, it's like sandbagging the Mississippi, or in my case, stacking it.

"If you think this is bad," I say, gesturing at the scattered piles, "you should see what you *don't* have to see."

Stacks are highly underrated as an organizing system. There's a natural selection to them. If I leave a stack long enough, coupons expire, sales circulars become outdated, deadlines slip by, and fundraisers end. It saves me a lot of trouble.

Paul says it's a mess.

"Not messy," I say. "Full of life."

Our active family launches from this house. It's not a museum; it's a work in progress. The kitchen table stack consists of a notebook for the writing class I teach, three baby pictures that fell off the refrigerator, a PTO membership application, Stephen's report card, the high school volleyball schedule, a checklist for setting financial goals, a review of a book called *Never Be Late Again*, an ad for a new yarn store, dinner menus from *Woman's Day* magazine, a hurricane preparedness guide, a recipe for artichoke dip, and my swim cap and goggles.

"We've got it going on," I say.

"I just want to see the counter," he pleads.

Each week I kid myself that I'm cleaning, but all I really do is shift stacks. "Life is about moving piles," my friend MJ says. I ricochet from surface to surface, sorting, shuffling, and recombining. There's actually no net reduction of paperwork, but it gives me a sense of accomplishment.

The funny thing is, when Paul walks in, he says, "You cleaned up. It looks nice." All I did was consolidate. Where there were once six stacks, I made two and lined up the corners.

I had an "aha" moment then. If I disinfected the kitchen so well he could perform surgery on the floor, he wouldn't care. He saw only clutter. This slight disconnect in the definition of clean caused a good deal of misunderstanding in our relationship.

I negotiated a marital détente. On the kitchen counter there is a big stack—the clutter zone. At great personal effort, Paul refrains from looking at it or complaining about it. In return, I contain my administrivia to one spot.

Sure, you can grow lab cultures in the sink. There's enough dust on the dresser to plow. But if the man of the house says it's clean, we have peace.

Wardrobe Malfunction

One Saturday afternoon as I headed home, our neighbor passed me on his motorcycle. This wasn't just any motorcycle; it was a limited edition Excelsior Henderson, all chrome and flash. He wore his black leather jacket and, for a moment, I thought I heard George Thorogood's "B-b-b-b b-a-a-d to the Bone" in the distance.

Then I pulled in to my driveway. Paul stood there in the oldest, dirtiest, greasiest, baggiest sweats he owned. He was unshowered, unshaved, and had his baseball hat on backwards to hide the bed head.

My man.

I laughed so hard I cried.

Paul is "wardrobe challenged."

Since he just reaches for an Army uniform during the week, dressing himself on weekends is a skill set he hasn't acquired. He's dependent on camouflage.

Now, with his broad shoulders and six-foot frame, he fills out the battle dress uniform (BDU) nicely. He does church clothes well, too; we bought a suit just for weddings and first communions. It's that vast spectrum of occasions between super sloppy and "dressed to the nines" that confounds him. I believe the current term is "smart casual." What does one wear to dinner with friends, or to a Hail and Farewell, or a sports banquet? He relies on his good pair of jeans, which is shorthand for saying they don't have paint on them.

"I don't know, honey," I said, checking him out before we left for the evening. He had on faded, too-long corduroys, a plaid shirt, and a shapeless beige sweater. I took his hand and said lovingly, "You look like a duffel bag."

"That does it," he said, flinging my arm aside. "Buy me some new clothes." He formally declared himself a salvage project. As far as men's fashions go, my expertise wasn't much better than his. With female clothing I can talk trends, accessories, hem lengths, and handbags. Renovating Paul represented a steep learning curve for us both.

We began by ruthlessly purging his closet. This was difficult for him, as he was emotionally attached to his surplus athletic wear. He kept resorting to the "functional" defense. Holding up a t-shirt he won at volleyball intramurals years before, he pronounced it, "stained but functional." "Frayed but functional," he said of Florida State shorts which were at least a decade old. "Torn but functional" was the verdict on a set of three-for-ten-dollar shirts he bought at a gas station.

"Those were seconds when you got them and now they really look like crap," I said, pitching them into the trash. I made a mental note to ransack his bureau in secret and carry everything directly to the dumpster. "Now let's get rid of these pants."

"I love those khakis!" he protested.

"Paul, I've mended them three times. Clothing has a natural life. It's time to let go." I pried his white knuckles away. "Same with this hideous mustard yellow bowling shirt."

"You bought that for me!"

"I did not! I'd remember that." Paul flinched as I tossed hanger after hanger. "This rugby jersey was from our first Christmas together. And I'm pretty sure you had that flannel button down in high school." When I finished, a suit and four sets of BDUs were left in the closet.

So much for the salvage. We began the restoration.

First of all, it involved parting with cash, which conflicted with his natural frugality. "You actually have to spend a little money to look nice," I coached him. For years he had remained ignorant, relying on Christmas gifts from me and his generous mother. Noting his alarm at the cost, I added reassuringly, "We'll do a little at a time."

I studied catalogs for looks. We knocked off ideas and formulated fashion guidelines, just like they do on TV's "What Not to Wear."

"Let's make you a little hipper," I said, pointing to a handsome model in a buttercup crewneck. "Do you like this?"

"Too preppy."

"How about this lambskin blazer?"

"Too expensive." He glanced at the paper sack of discarded clothes.

Change is hard.

"Come on. Let's figure out how to make the most of your V-shaped body, soldier."

Slowly we accumulated crisp shirts in rich, assertive hues like burgundy, indigo, and paprika. The threadbare white undershirts went away and were replaced with charcoal and flax colored t-shirts to add interest at the collar. Tired khakis found new owners at the Goodwill Store, and we bought creased, custom-hemmed trousers. He got a spiffy belt, matching socks, and grown-up shoes. To top it off, I found a textured sports jacket that complemented any of his shirts.

The final understated results suited him well. Everything worked together; he just opened his closet to a range of choices.

"You look so handsome," I said, as he came downstairs before our date wearing black pants and a Perry Ellis sweater, "and you dressed yourself!"

"Don't talk to me like I'm a three-year old," he said.

"Sorry," I quickly added. "You don't have to take my word for it. Shelly saw you at the hockey game, and she said you looked really together."

He beamed. The salvage project was complete.

Fisherman Husband

Ever since Paul got assigned to Rhode Island, we've felt like an immigrant species to the local population. New England may be the home of the NFL's Patriots, but Army folks are like alien life forms here. Unlike those well-known southern towns ending in "ville"—Fayetteville, Hinesville, Leesville, and Clarksville—people in BDUs are few and far between.

Being the "Ocean State," Rhode Island has a strong Navy tradition, but Rhode Islanders freely admit they don't understand Army people. They want to know what makes us tick. What do we think? How do we act?

Thanks to a lot of unflattering portrayals from Hollywood through the years, many uninformed citizens still think soldiers are a few steps behind on the evolutionary ladder. "You seem to be one of the smarter ones," a university colleague thoughtlessly remarked to Paul. With his poise and education Paul has challenged a lot of the military stereotypes in this college community, which still retains a lot of Vietnam-era backwash.

In neighboring Massachusetts, a friend of ours recently attended his high school reunion. Since graduating from the U.S. Military Academy two decades ago, he has done great things in the Army. He commanded a battalion in Afghanistan with Operation Anaconda. A colonel now, he has been promoted ahead of his peers three times. Overlooking those accomplishments, his hometown classmates asked, "Why are you still in the Army? Couldn't you find a better job?"

I'd like to think what they're really asking is, "Why would you choose to be an infantryman? Why would you sleep in the dirt, wade through the mud, carry hundred pound rucksacks on your back, and cover yourself with green paint? For God's sakes, isn't there an easier way to make a living?"

The short answer is that some are hard-wired for the physical demands of this warrior life. Their DNA practically dictates it, and they find it enormously satisfying. The more complicated response is that Paul works for what he believes—the security and safety of the United States. He identifies strongly with his role as a defender. That's the only way he could spring out of bed at 5:30 a.m. and leave for physical training when it's still dark outside. On deployments, he routinely works weeks with no time off, but he stays focused. His sense of purpose comes from dedication to duty and love of country.

When I clerked at a bookstore, I asked another employee what she thought about my suggestions to improve the check out. She yawned and said, "I don't get emotionally involved. I just want my paycheck."

That's the difference between her and people like Paul. He *is* emotionally involved. He works for more than the next paycheck.

"It's not what I do. It's who I am." Those words, overheard at a party, could have been Paul's. Instead, they came from a commercial fisherman in Rhode Island. Like the Army, it's a difficult vocation. They leave their families for weeks or months to go to sea. The work is strenuous and sometimes deadly. They're at the mercy of the ocean, weather, and hazards on the boat. After all that, commercial fishing often doesn't even pay well.

In spite of the arguments for finding a more stable job, fishermen still say, "I wouldn't choose anything else." The heart has its reasons. It's the same for Paul. While at Fort Campbell, the children and I drove Paul on post for his deployment to the Balkans. As he saluted the gate guard smartly, I noticed a new patch on his shoulder. It was an American flag, but the stars were in the wrong corner.

"Why is it backwards?" I said.

"Picture a flag bearer in battle," Paul explained. "He's charging forward so the stars come first. It's meant to show we never retreat."

With great strength and commitment, he has served his country for over 20 years. Adlai Stevenson, Jr. said, "Patriotism is not a short and frenzied outburst of emotion but the tranquil and steady dedication of a lifetime." Paul feels that calling in every cell of his body.

Whenever any of my New England friends quiz me about his chosen profession, I explain it with familiar examples.

"Like those fishermen," I begin. Pretty soon they understand. Fishermen fish, and soldiers soldier. It's who they are.

CNN Commando

"Your dad wants to go to war, but they won't let him," Daniel said to Stephen. "That's what I heard." Our ten-year old nephew didn't get it quite right, but he was close. In 20 years with the Army, Paul had the misfortune, he says, of missing all the action, starting with the Grenada invasion in 1983 when he was a cadet at West Point.

"I've never been in combat," Paul regrets, "but I've watched a lot of it on TV." He jokes about being a "CNN commando with several oak leaf clusters."

Although he jokes about it, he's disappointed. To him, good luck is getting that call in the middle of the night: "Wheels up in 18 hours." He's still waiting for the phone to ring.

So rather than retire at age 42, Paul requested an assignment to Afghanistan or Iraq for a year.

"Why'd he do that?" my civilian neighbor asked. "He can just get out." Paul lives under the warrior's ethos. "If our guys are out there fighting," he says, "that's where I need to be too."

I saw this early in our marriage. Ever since 1989, when I mention that Paul served in the First Ranger Battalion, I hear, "Really? Did he go to Panama?"

"No."

"I bet he was mad."

"He was."

He and several other newly promoted captains had been reassigned to Fort Benning in November. Operation Just Cause, the airfield seizure which they had rehearsed, happened a month later. Jumping into Panama was a "warrior's dream come true," Paul told me, a chance to prove himself under combat conditions. Missing it by 30 days was enough reason to have an extended pity party at Fort Benning.

It was our first Christmas together so I was glad he didn't go.

He wanted to be in a Third World country searching for Manuel Noriega with the troops. Instead, he was drinking eggnog with me.

"I feel like the 12th man," he said.

Later that day I was baking zucchini bread for gifts and saw him doing yard work. He looked so forlorn that I went out to cheer him up.

"Don't ever tell me men and women are the same," he growled. "We want to be saving the world and you want us here raking."

Not many wives would say they eagerly look forward to their husband's departure to a combat zone. After several weeks of listening to him whine, however, I made an offer.

"Why don't I charter a plane and fly you to Central America myself?"

He was insufferable as an armchair infantryman. Sadly for both of us, he's had more opportunities to practice it. His peacekeeping mission to Kosovo, he maintains, didn't count. During Operation Desert Storm Paul was assigned to a non-deployable unit. When Operations Enduring Freedom and Iraqi Freedom began, he was non-deployable in an ROTC position.

"I've kept the university safe during the Global War on Terror," he declared to two of his contemporaries, who've experienced similar timing during their tenure in the Army.

"I saw privates with combat patches at Fort Campbell," one lieutenant colonel countered.

"The plebe class at West Point has 30 combat veterans from Iraq," another replied. "Face it guys, we're the back-ups."

But the second string isn't heading to the bus in resignation and defeat. They're pacing like caged animals. They're marching to the sound of the guns.

The Fiery Re-entry

"I want a man in my life but not in my house."
—Joy Behar, "The View"

I was reading in the family room when Paul clomped by on his way to the garage. The door slammed behind him. He came back in. SLAM! A few minutes later, he walked by again. SLAM! He returned. SLAM! I closed my book and moved.

I turned the ignition in my minivan and the radio blared out a sports talk show at top volume. The seat adjustments were all wrong; the rearview mirror was askew.

I can't sleep diagonally in the bed anymore.

The signs were all there: the "fiery re-entry" period had begun.

"It's infinitely easier to run the house and make decisions when the 'alpha dog' is not around," a friend emailed me. What happens when the alpha dog returns? All hell breaks loose. That's the fiery re-entry.

Spacecraft returning to earth's atmosphere generate friction and heat up to 3000 degrees. If it weren't designed to withstand such violent temperatures, the shuttle would vaporize. It's a harsh but apt metaphor for what happens when our military men rejoin the family.

The Army Center for Health Promotion once distributed decks of playing cards with wellness tips printed on them. The six of diamonds read, "Coming Home: Expect changes. Spouse and children may be more independent."

What an understated way to describe such a tortured transition. For an uncensored version, consider this note from a friend after her husband returned from Iraq.

"B. is home for good to bug us all daily! I can't begin to

explain the readjustment we are going through. I thought we had this stuff figured out, but this one is the WORST! I am very thankful he is out of harm's way, but if he keeps up the attitude, I'm gonna have to kick his ass!!"

Despite the romantic, rose-colored expectations we have, reunions are often amped-up exercises in finding each other's emotional buttons. During three years of successive absences at Fort Campbell, Paul and I learned more coping skills than we ever thought necessary. Each time he came home, it felt like he was butting in. The first 24 to 48 hours were the worst. Paul was often ham-handed in his approach, and I was hair-trigger impatient.

"Where are the bills that were on the table?" I once asked.

"Were they in a manila envelope?" said Paul.

"Yes."

"I put it on the top shelf in the upstairs closet," he said.

"Did you think to ask me? Maybe I had a plan for it. You know, I managed everything while you were gone. I guess I'll just go *drool* on myself now."

The Reunion Training booklet offered this advice: "Use 'I' statements. They won't put your partner on the defensive, and the dialogue will be more productive."

We tried that technique when he came home one Friday.

"I wish you were still gone!"

"I wish I were still gone, too!"

Not our finest hour.

Paul and I were still circling each other when he left again on Sunday. We parted on bad terms and I felt awful.

"I hope nothing happens to him while he's gone," I said. We had to make our peace again. Eventually, we did.

When we could laugh about our conflicts, I knew the heat shields were in place for his re-entry. Before he returned from six months in the Balkans, we exchanged these emails:

Dear Marna,

I've started the mental process of reintegration with the family. Let me see, if I remember from past experience. When I get home I need to re-establish my position as the leader of the household. Expect me to immediately exert my influence over everything from grocery shopping to financial management to the proper way to do laundry. And if that's not enough, then I'll expect you to feel sorry for me for being away from the comforts of home on such a hardship assignment!

So much for humor! As you and I both know, all of the above is exactly what I will not be doing! I know there will be some reintegration hiccups, but I also know I'm too experienced at this (by now) to make the catastrophic errors that I cluelessly committed in the past.

Dear Paul,

Here are some suggestions for when you get home.

Pretend like you are a guest in the house for a few days.

Ask what you can do to help.

Compliment your wife all the time.

Offer to take the family out to dinner.

Unload the dishwasher.

Do the laundry.

Take out the trash without being reminded.

Consider weekly pre-emptive flower strikes.

Let me sleep diagonally in the bed.

Say "I'm sorry" every morning when you wake up.

Your loving wife,

Household 6

P.S. I forgive you.

Hiking and Dancing

It looks like hiking, but we're dancing.

Sure, I'm wearing treaded boots as I huff up this 3000-foot mountain. I stop about every 25 yards to catch my breath and take a drink. Elena and Stephen, tired of waiting, have scampered ahead and are probably scaling the summit by now. Only Paul remains, carrying the trail mix, handing me water, wiping my brow.

"I thought you said a short hike, Paul?"

"It's short. Only two and a half miles."

"But it's straight up!"

Just then a couple walks by and I overhear the woman say, "I hiked to the top of this mountain on my sixth birthday."

Okay, if a kindergartner did it, I can do it. We clamber over boulders again, making our way to the top. It looks like hiking but we're dancing. This is the dance of marriage, the dance of compromise, the dance of understanding. I prefer long walks on flat and preferably paved paths with comfort stations at regular intervals. Paul loves the rugged hikes. Even though he's an infantryman in the Army and gets plenty of time in the field, he's still an outdoorsman. He likes nothing more than taking off for a campground with plenty of trails nearby. It's not as much fun to me as, say, a spa weekend, but because he loves it, I tuck my air mattress in the van and go. I'm a good sport, but I have my limits.

Several years ago Paul was preparing for a weeklong hike on the Appalachian Trail with his father and brother. His backpack was stuffed to seam-splitting capacity with food, clothes, and shelter.

"Let me put this on," I said. "I want to see how heavy it is."

He hoisted the pack onto my back and I momentarily lost my balance. With great strain, I regained it and lurched forward, managing one half-step before momentum crushed me to the ground.

Paul rushed over where I lay pinned and helpless, feet flailing skyward like a stunned cockroach. He quickly freed me from the strangling weight.

"You're carrying that thing around for five days?" I said. "Looks like a whole lot of backache to me."

"What would it take to get you out on the trail with me?" he asked.

"Do they have one of those services where they go ahead with all the heavy stuff and set up camp?" I asked between attempts to catch my breath. "I just carry a fanny pack and show up in time for dinner. Do they have those?"

"You mean a Sherpa?"

"Is that what they're called?"

"Yes, but no. They don't allow llamas on the Appalachian Trail," he patiently explained.

"Too bad," I said. "They should."

Paul had post-retirement visions of us strolling through the Smoky Mountains arm-in-arm. That's not going to happen. I get grouchy living off Vienna sausages, and I like a hot shower every 24 hours. If he wants to rough it in the forest primeval, he hooks up with his Army friends.

Instead, Paul and I adjust and accommodate. I agree to day hikes, which is why we are scaling Mount Monadnock in New Hampshire. After reaching the peak, I stumble down the slope, winging from tree to tree, knees and thighs throbbing. Wordless, I fall into our tent and crash for an hour.

It looks like hiking, but we're dancing. Next time, when I suggest a home tour or a symphony, he won't dismiss me, and we'll waltz our way through it together.

Motherhood

Military families are young and have young children. Parenting is a frenzied business, but when you factor in a nomadic life, government quarters, new schools and new friends, limited pay, and a father who departs soon after the birth of a baby, the antics border on the absurd. Let's call it, "modern motherhood on speed."

Sick Call

I was in New Mexico at my younger sister's wedding when I got a phone message from Paul. He was at home in New York taking care of our two children.

"Stephen doesn't feel good. His temperature is a hundred and one degrees. What should I do? Call me back."

I immediately telephoned. "Give him Tylenol. Have him drink lots of water. Take his temperature again. Go to the doctor if that doesn't help." It sounded like Stephen had a virus—nothing major—but my three-year old was sick and his mommy was two thousand miles away.

My mother, seeing my unease muttered, "I don't know why Paul told you. What can you do about it here?"

Every chance I got I called home. "How's Stephen?"

"The same," Paul reported wearily. "I took him outside this afternoon. We sat in the front yard. He just wants to be held. He slept a lot."

"Did you go to the doctor?"

"No. Maria took his temperature and it was normal again." Maria was our nosy and somewhat neurotic neighbor.

"That's good," I said.

"You know what?" Paul said. "I haven't gotten a thing done since you left."

"That's a shame," I said peevishly.

When I returned after the weekend, Stephen was the picture of health again as he kicked the soccer ball with the other kids.

The next day, I stood outside with a few ladies from the neighborhood. Maria said to me, "Marna, we decided that we're not going to listen to you when you complain about how tired you are. I mean, after the weekend Paul had ..."

"Excuse me?"

After the weekend Paul had?

I was dumbstruck. I didn't trust myself to reply without saying something mean, so I stormed off to the backyard. My forehead pinched in fury, I grabbed a hoe and hacked at the weeds in my garden. I had been talking to myself for awhile before I noticed another neighbor standing at my gate.

"Have you had enough of Maria yet?" Ellen said.

"Don't get me started," I said. "I've taken care of sick children by myself many times. I drove Elena to the emergency room in the middle of the night once. Stephen had the chicken pox while Paul was in the field."

My forceful swipes to the soil left huge gashes in the ground. I was on a roll.

"Hasn't Maria ever heard of Murphy's Law? The baby was colicky for two months while Paul was at a staff course. One night there was no heat in the house." I paused to wipe dirt from my forehead. "They repaired the upstairs radiator, and then it leaked into our kitchen light. We could have been electrocuted!"

I felt so victimized I practically dug a trench next to the tomatoes.

I recalled how a thunderstorm wrapped our shed around a tree while Paul was away. A power surge shorted the TV, microwave, and VCR. Another time, our truck quit while I was driving at night in the rain. A blizzard dumped a foot of snow just hours after Paul departed. Then the whole household fell ill from a bug for which there's no English pronunciation.

"You've had it so much worse," Ellen said sympathetically.

Ah, a true friend in my corner. And thanks to Maria, my garden was ready for fall planting.

Micro-Soccer Mom

I vaguely remember saying, "If you really can't find someone, I could probably do it." My fate was sealed. Within a week the league manager phoned.

"You're my last hope. Without you, we won't have enough coaches."

"But I don't know how to coach soccer," I protested. "I only played intramurals in college and that was twenty years ago."

"We'll teach you everything," she said. "There's a workshop this Saturday."

That's how I became coach for the Jaguars—a micro-soccer team of four-year olds. Fine work for someone who didn't know a corner kick from a drop kick.

Panic-stricken, I attended the coaching clinic at the high school, scribbling notes furiously. I asked lots of questions and pursued every scenario. I felt like an imposter.

The first day of practice, I armed myself with all the accessories. I wore a whistle around my neck and a knit shirt with "Coach" embroidered on it. I brought balls, cones, a first aid kit, and an air pump. I looked the part, but it soon became obvious to everyone that I was a rookie. My session was way too complicated.

"Kick the ball to each other!" I shouted, clutching my clipboard. "Dribble between the cones! Where are my defenders?"

"I'll stand here," offered one dad, stationing himself at the end of the field and capturing runaway players.

"Why don't you just take my job?" I gasped, but my voice was lost in the windy field. When the last child left I collapsed. There had to be a better way.

I borrowed a video from the library on drills for the micro-soccer set.

"Keep it fun," said the narrator with an endearing British accent. "The most important thing at this age is familiarization with the sport." He outlined a simple 45-minute practice session. It was suddenly so obvious—I needed to lighten up.

Fun became the guiding principle. Warm-ups consisted of running after my players, trying to kick the ball away as they squealed with delight. We did dribbling relays. I promised "birdie sips" to the winners.

"Birdie sips, birdie sips," they chanted, as I lined them up and squirted water from my sports bottle into their open mouths.

When the season began, I found that micro-soccer had its own rhythm that no coaching could alter. It was "herd ball," plain and simple. My whole team was clueless, and totally adorable. They couldn't even keep track of which goal was theirs.

The comical scenes kept me in stitches each week. One girl lost interest in a scoring attempt and sat down to blow fronds off a dandelion. Another skipped up and down the field the entire game. Someone else chased a butterfly. A boy decided that the running around was simply too tiring and retreated to the side-lines mid-play. One child got knocked down and burst into tears at the indignity. A team daddy brushed him off and gingerly carried him from the field.

Once Stephen spied a hill just beyond the goal and decided to roll down it. His teammates followed and soon they were all tumbling and giggling in the grass.

"Let's take a break and sort this out," the official suggested. "It's almost half-time anyway." There were two critical moments during a micro-soccer match: oranges at half-time and power snacks after the game. Everything else was just filler.

When soccer ended, I asked Stephen to tell me his favorite part of the season.

"The pizza party when I got my trophy," he said.

I liked that I got to keep my "Coach" shirt. I may have been the one with the whistle, but the Jaguars were my teachers. They reminded me to skip around, catch butterflies, roll down hills, and above all, eat.

Rainbow Chasing

One afternoon in Tennessee, we were driving around with time to kill between soccer practice and piano lessons when we spotted a rainbow.

"Let's see if we can find where it ends," I said to Elena and Stephen. It looked like it might be right over the hill in the next neighborhood.

We snaked our way through the subdivision, driving down a street, then doubling back when it dead-ended. I tried alternate routes. In a slow and meandering fashion, we moved in the general direction of the rainbow.

"We should be there by now!" a frustrated Elena yelled.

After wandering through the development, we finally arrived at the boundary of the neighborhood where the roads stopped. I pulled off to the side so we could get a panoramic view of the rainbow.

"This is as close as we're going to get gang," I said. The luminous spectrum dipped behind the backyard creek and disappeared over a rise. The sky beyond the ridge glimmered with a surreal light. Elena and Stephen delighted in the outcome of our adventure.

"Mom," Stephen asked, "have you ever seen the end of a rainbow?"

In fact, I had seen one when I was a helicopter pilot in the Army years before. I was flying during a deployment to Honduras. We were about four hundred feet off the ground and had just flown through a late afternoon shower. The rainbow swept from left to right across our view. I was thrilled because we were going to fly right by the end of the arc. I was actually going to see that enchanted spot where leprechauns tossed gold coins.

I was so intently searching the ground for the rainbow's end that I almost missed it entirely. The rainbow didn't connect to the earth, but stopped in mid-air. At ninety knots, we whizzed by the light and water equivalent of a "poof." The mythical site was nothing but a diffuse, misty evaporation: perishable and no more tangible than a batch of soap bubbles.

"Have you, Mom?" Stephen interrupted my reminiscing.

I looked at his face, precious and innocent. "Yes, I've seen the end of a rainbow," I said. He moved closer to me.

"Was there a pot of gold?" He brimmed with excitement. This was the kindergartner who rigged up leprechaun traps made of shoe boxes and aluminum foil on St. Patrick's Day. What was I supposed to say? "No, honey, everything you've heard is a lie. There's no gold, no shamrocks, no little green men—it's all a figment of someone's imagination. Sorry about that, kid."

Or should I make up some colorful scenario to match the tales he'd heard? I decided I shouldn't attempt storytelling on-the-fly. At least with Santa Claus and the Tooth Fairy I could parrot centuries of cultural half-truths. I didn't trust myself to fabricate Celtic falsehoods. Stephen and Elena would see through it.

I decided to tell them the truth and brace myself for the anguish.

"No," I said carefully. "I didn't see a pot of gold at the end of the rainbow."

He and Elena considered this revelation. How I hated being the instrument of their disappointment. It was a heartbreakingly cruel parent moment.

Stephen slumped. Elena looked away and I felt like a creep. Suddenly, Stephen perked up.

"It must have been at the other end!" he decided.

I laughed with relief. Of course! Only one pot of gold per rainbow. Elena and Stephen were completely satisfied with that explanation. My contracted heart swelled with joy again.

With the magnificent rainbow glowing over our heads, we drove to piano.

What was at the other end of that rainbow in Honduras? Only the leprechauns know for sure.

Emotional Distance

Paul and I have different rhythms when it comes to life's transitions.

"Can we toss these?" he asked, holding up a collection of paper plate art from Elena's preschool days.

I can't answer under duress.

"Let me think about it. I need some emotional distance," I said.

"Emotional distance. That's a good one," he said. "It's just a yes-or-no question." He carefully placed the masterpieces in a box. In time I may part with them, or I may not. They had sentimental value to me, and there's no rational answer to that.

There's one item he doesn't even ask about anymore: the blue stroller. With each move, he wordlessly hauls the contraption up and down the basement stairs. It's seen the Cherry Blossom festival, nine homes, and every shopping mall in the mid-Atlantic states. We pushed two babies through their childhoods in it. Even though my baby is now eleven, I don't have the "emotional distance" to get rid of the stroller. I suspect it will be stowed, at the ready, when our grandchildren visit.

When Stephen was four we staged the watershed yard sale. We weren't having any more children so we sold the baby equipment. When our neighbors saw the gates and swings, the changing table, booster seat, and Johnny Jump-up all for sale, we heard many superstitious comments.

"That's the best fertility medicine there is."

"Next week, you'll find out you're pregnant again."

We couldn't keep everything, but I started a "save" pile. Some of the clothes and booties for newborns were just too cute! I remembered the two-week period when my babies wore them— their sweet faces, their cottony-clean smell. I got misty just thinking about it. Now there's a bag of Onesies next to the stroller, gathering emotional distance.

The next rite of passage was the Little Tikes stage—those big, brightly colored, plastic toys. We bought the Country Cottage for Elena when she was eighteen months old, and she played in it for years. At various times, it was her apartment, club house, and snack bar. She even requested a potted plant for the front stoop.

"I'm 'making cooking,'" she said through the window, stirring the bucket full of water, soil, sticks, and leaves.

"Dirt soup," I said. "It looks yummy!"

When she quit keeping house and wanted to slide down the roof into the wading pool below, it was time to direct her to more physical pursuits. She started soccer.

Although Stephen never set up housekeeping in the Country Cottage, the engineering marvel of a door on hinges captivated him. As a two-year old, he'd occupy himself for 20 minutes going in and out. When he got a little older he tried to scale the house like Spiderman.

He was about four when he lost interest in the Country Cottage and the orange Cozy Coupe as well. The baby swing had long since been mothballed. The climbing cube and slide sat abandoned in the backyard. Both children moved on, and the days of them sticking Cheetos up their noses were behind us. "Keep or throw?" Paul asked, pointing to the cottage. I resisted. "We can get rid of these now," he said.

Word got out that Little Tikes toys were for sale—there was always a good market for those on post. People called with offers. Soon we had buyers for everything. Delighted mothers with trucks and minivans carted away my precious memories while Paul counted the cash. I stood on the curb, fighting back the tears. Now I understand why women get pregnant one last time. The transitions are too gut-wrenching.

"Semper Gumby!"

As a preschooler, Elena knew the drill at Kinder Gym class. It started with free play on the mats and equipment. Then a bell rang and they had circle sing-along, followed by a few more minutes of jumping around. When the exit jingle began, the leader blew some bubbles, and then each child got a clown stamp on the way out. In forty-five minutes, the charming routine was over, and Elena was content.

Consistency is everything at that age. At 43, I still have a toddler's heart. I crave a consistent schedule. This is not something a military wife can reasonably expect to have. The Army, by its nature, keeps us off balance. The commissary layout is shuffled just when we have it figured out. Battalions and companies reorganize under new names. Deployment dates shift.

"*Semper gumby!*" That's the battle cry of the military wife— "always flexible." We must be able to expertly manage a life of constant adjustments. False starts, back tracking, and second guessing shouldn't bother us. In reality, they make us feel like a pooch during a particularly bad flea-and-tick season.

Structure, not shift-on-the-fly, works best for me. Often during our marriage Paul was deployed. Even when he was home his workdays began before dawn and finished fourteen hours later. *His* schedule was a constant. Although solo parenting was challenging for me, I planned my day and paced myself. With babysitters, carpools, and friends in place, I handled it.

Compared to the grueling regimen of a line unit, Paul had banker's hours when he attended a year-long course at Fort Leavenworth, Kansas. I expected an easier go of it, but it was still stressful. Our neighbor gave me an explanation.

"Predictability is more important than presence," he said. "We finally figured it out."

Predictability *is* more important than presence. That was

why there was such upheaval in the house. There was no routine or plan to our days. I couldn't get into a groove. Yes, Paul's time at home increased, but it was scattershot: a half hour in the morning, a quick lunch at home, dinner with the family more often. We passed each other coming and going, but it was like death by duck bites. Duck in, duck out … no two days were the same.

One morning, as I finished the breakfast dishes, Paul pulled in.

"Class was rescheduled," he said. "We're having a seminar tonight instead."

"But you were supposed to take Stephen to soccer."

"I can't now. You'll have to drop Elena off at piano for me, too."

"Great," I said, "that means my yoga class is out of the question."

"I'm real sorry about that, hon'. By the way, tomorrow afternoon we've got a study group, so I can't go to the commissary. And remember, I'm writing my paper this weekend." He disappeared up the stairs and returned in shorts and Nike shoes.

"I'm going running," he said, right before I threw the wet dishrag at him.

He gave me presence, but no predictability, just transitions, contingencies, and interruptions. There was no worry-free delegating. I was perpetually on-call to accommodate changes.

Deployments, unaccompanied tours, and train-ups were non-negotiable. I did what I needed to do. I bet most military wives prefer those fixed states over crazy non-schedules. When at the mercy of those, it's like trying to catch money blowing around inside a phone booth—a lot of work just to grab a buck or two.

After I had fetched Elena from her friend's house, quickly made dinner, dressed Stephen for practice, packed a snack bag, and loaded the car, Paul called.

"I finished work early. I can take Stephen to soccer after all."

That's why I'm slumped on the floor, humming the song from Kinder Gym. It was the last time I knew what was coming next.

My Kingdom for a Babysitter

At 3:10 in the afternoon, my friend Sarah and I were sitting on her front porch watching the middle schoolers step off their bus. Although we weren't crouched in the bushes, we were as serious as detectives on a stake-out.

"What have you got?" I asked, squinting for a better look.

"I see two at twelve o'clock and one at nine o'clock," she replied.

"I'm out of here," I vaulted over the flower bed, narrowly missing a trio of preschool boys playing Matchbox cars. "I'll follow the pair, you get the single," I yelled. One subject disappeared into a set of quarters, and I jotted down her address, a description, and the last name next to the door. If she passed muster, she was mine. I did the same thing for the other girl.

Sarah met me back at the porch. We had a debriefing.

"Two promising prospects," I said. "Their backpacks were full. They must be good students."

"Mine, too," she said. "We're bound to get a decent babysitter out of the three of them."

This was the Mommy Meat Market. Normally, I handled this mission alone. Parents on military posts considered information about babysitters "Top Secret." The better sitters were so safe they could be in the Witness Protection Program. I usually didn't share my list, but Sarah and I agreed to pool resources.

It's kid central in military housing. We're all in the thick of raising our 2.4 children; we drive minivans with Froot-Loop crusted car seats. Because our husbands are in the same line of work, we have parallel social calendars, too. If there's a reception or a Military Ball, many of us scramble to get sitters from a small pool of teenagers. Some folks call weeks, even months, in advance. An acquaintance tried to put a babysitter on retainer for the whole season.

"There's no such thing!" I informed her. "It's a dog-eat-dog world out there. I'll start a bidding war if necessary."

To keep them happy and to earn preferential treatment, I bribed my babysitters. The good ones received an obscene hourly rate.

"Think how many spaghetti strap tops just one evening of work could buy," I said. I offered top pay and a comprehensive "benefits" package—sodas, snacks, videos, and premium cable.

I also recruited sitters aggressively. Paul said my tactics bordered on assault. I interrogated teenagers at church, the PX, and the pool.

"Excuse me," I said blocking their escape path. "How old are you, and do you babysit?"

Stephen and I were at the playground when two older girls rolled by on skates. I pursued them on foot. Another time, I asked a college-aged waitress at the officer's club if she babysat.

"No," she said, "but I get asked that all the time."

After collecting potential candidates, a good babysitter was still hard to find. Once I came home to a 16-year old asleep in front of the television. The living room was a wreck and the dinner dishes were still on the table. Elena confirmed my impression.

"I didn't like her. She drew on my picture," she said the next morning.

On the other hand, the blonde girl who lived across the street arrived with her mother the first time because the 12-year old was "In Training." After being entertained with games and modeling clay all evening, Elena and Stephen kept asking, "When's Kerry coming over again?"

The biggest coup was finding a babysitter who drove herself to my house. Ideally, I would have a sixteen year old girl with a car who, when called by someone else, would telephone and say, "The so-and-so's asked me to babysit, and I wanted to make sure you didn't need me. You're my priority after all." First dibs, that's all I asked.

Ah, a mother's fantasy … For now I had to maintain sanity until my daughter turned twelve. Then I'd have a live-in babysitter I could use to the fullest extent of the current Child Labor Laws.

"I Miss Dad"

One morning after my sixth grader Elena left for the bus, I realized she forgot her lunch. I grabbed it and jogged to the end of the road to catch her. What I saw put a sad knot in my stomach. Three girls stood at the bus stop talking and laughing. Elena was sitting by herself, reading. No one was making an effort to include the new girl.

I was so upset I called my friend Tracy when I got home.

"Are we scarring her for life?" I ranted. "Is it time to stop moving around?"

"She was reading?" Tracy said. "Maybe that's what she wanted to do."

"But they weren't paying any attention to her," I raced on.

"They're probably a bunch of bitchy teens," Tracy said. "You know middle school girls. Elena made a good choice."

With twenty years as an Army wife and four children, Tracy has seen every age and stage. "Our children have always been the number one concern when we talked about continuing with the military," she told me. "So far, they're doing okay."

But her oldest, Ashley, had just started high school, and Tracy was having doubts. She was still smarting from the soccer coach's recent comment to her freshman daughter.

"You won't get to play much here," he told her. "I've got to put in the girls that are going to be around next year."

The frequency of their moves, Tracy said, would put Ashley in a new high school right before senior year. During the decision on whether to stay in the Army, they gave her a worst-case scenario.

"You might not have any friends at first."

"I'll be okay," she said.

"You might have to eat alone at lunch."

"Don't worry about me, Mom."

But military parents do worry. When I've asked Elena about relocating she says, "I like moving." On the other hand, during her drama queen moments, she'll scream, "I never have any friends."

It's hard to sort out the crisis-du-jour from true emotional pain. For example, another friend of mine was told by the middle school guidance counselor, "I don't know how your son gets through the day. He has no friends at all." Now that's heartbreaking.

As an Army mother, I hope my children have a knack for fitting in, but I'm vigilant about their feelings in this matter. It's tough being the new kid. Heck, it's tough to be the new adult! When Elena and Stephen were young, I worried that having their father gone so much created problems. First-time parenthood coincided with an especially intense period of Paul's infantry career—company command. He was often gone for weeks at a time. When he left, I told Elena how many "sleeps" until he got home.

"Mom," my toddler declared after breakfast, "you said Dad would be home in six sleeps and it's been six sleeps."

"No, honey, it's only been two. We have four more sleeps to go."

"Oh." She chewed her cereal thoughtfully. "Can I go to bed now?"

She missed him but was easily diverted with playgrounds and cookies, or so I thought.

After Paul changed command we moved to Tallahassee, where he went to graduate school. He was around more to take Elena to preschool, the park, or the convenience store for Slushees. I couldn't believe the change in her.

"She's so much calmer now that Paul's home," I commented to my friend Lynn. Our husbands, both in the Army, attended classes together and we were tailgating before a Florida State University football game. It was a beautiful fall afternoon, yet

Lynn's two-year old son cried and whimpered in his dad's arms.

"Is he upset about something?" I asked.

"It's all these people walking by," Lynn explained, pointing at the fans on their way to the stadium. "Phillip thinks they're going bye-bye, and it reminds him of Dad leaving." They had just returned from a strenuous tour in Germany where Mike, his dad, was in the field most of the time. Young as he was, Phillip had been traumatized by the frequent absences.

Maybe young children suffered more than I realized. They picked up on the loneliness, the changed household, the keyed-up mom, the ever-so-subtle abandonment. Every military parent regularly asks, "Is it time to stop moving around?" The other question we ponder is what this lifestyle does to the kids.

"Are we scarring her for life?" I repeated, after seeing Elena at the bus stop.

"Or teaching her how to be resilient?" Tracy replied. Her daughter Ashley seemed to be facing the social challenges with poise and equanimity. Perhaps Elena will too. Meanwhile, I'll watch and worry.

Mom Job

"Don't bid on anything, Marna," Paul said, as he glanced up from balancing the checkbook. I was leaving to attend the elementary school's annual auction. Already I had spent too much money on a ticket just to get in the exclusive beach club where the fundraiser was being held.

"Right, dear." I blew him a goodbye kiss. Of course, I studied all sixty of the silent auction items, and submitted bids on several. At the end of the evening, I was the proud owner of two tickets to the U.S Open Golf Tournament in Newport, Rhode Island.

"Don't sweat the price, honey," I said when I showed them to Paul. "I used my own money."

Along with our household checking account into which Paul's monthly pay flows, I also have an account. I work as a receptionist for a local chiropractor. Two mornings each week, starting at seven, I check in patients, take co-payments, and reschedule appointments. Paul sees the kids off to school. I finish by 10 a.m. when the chiropractor leaves for his main office in another town.

"Aren't you a little overqualified for this job?" someone asked me, citing my master's degree and teaching credentials.

"It's a mom job," I answered. There are times in a woman's life when this employment is just right. My friend, Amy, clerks retail during the school day. Laura hostesses the lunch shifts at a downtown restaurant.

Mom jobs are not career tracks, nor are they very demanding. They require no daily preparation, and no stress follows me home. I only have to show up prepared to work. My part-time occupation provides me with socialization and stimulation. Without much additional craziness, my week gains a little structure from the sinkhole of errands and chores. I dress semi-professionally, instead of padding around in warm-ups all day. Best of all, every month money trickles into my checking account.

Not much, mind you, but a couple of hundred dollars that's all mine. This small sum is immune from standard marital negotiations. If I want to get a facial, buy a second bathing suit, or highlight my hair, I don't justify it at financial meetings. It's my own non-appropriated fund.

Paul recently designed a new family budget. At the top, he put his monthly income, and with fewer zeros, my contribution.

"Wait a minute," I said. "You can't do that. That's my money. That doesn't go to the electric bill."

"It's all our money," Paul said quietly, punching the calculator.

"No, that's mine."

"The money I make is our money, but the money you make is your money? Why is that, Marna?"

"It's just one of those things you have to accept," I said.

Fortunately for me, on that same day the advice column in the newspaper addressed a similar situation. A man wrote: "My wife stays home with the children. She does a few odd jobs and makes several thousand dollars a year. Yet she thinks of this as her money. Am I wrong to think this is unfair?"

I cut the article out and with my highlighter circled the most important sentence: "In a word, yes."

Look at what your wife has forfeited to set aside career for family, the columnist explained: pension credits, Social Security, up-to-date job skills, employability.

"You have these benefits," she told the husband. "Think of this as 'your' money. Meanwhile, your wife has taken time off to raise the kids. Let her spend the few thousand dollars a year. This is 'her' money."

I couldn't have said it better myself. In fact, she introduced reasons I had never considered.

One of my friends, a teacher, read the clipping on my refrigerator and disagreed. "My paycheck has always gone into the household fund," she said. Since she and her husband both worked outside the home because of mutual financial goals, they pooled resources. Her full-time paycheck brought equal status as a wage earner, which was a different dynamic than in my marriage.

Since Elena was born fifteen years ago, I stayed home to raise her and our son, Stephen. The emotional security in my children now has made my choice of full-time mothering worthwhile, but my contributions weren't financial.

My demanding position without pay, promotions, bonuses, or vacation days took a toll on my self-esteem. Many of our marital disagreements sprang from my expenditures on self care, like massages or clothing that Paul didn't think were necessary. His objections left me feeling unappreciated. Since I have my own money now, we've eliminated a lot of touchy bargaining. It doesn't come up at all, and that's a good thing. If I want something and he doesn't agree, I say, "I'll pay for it," and harmony is restored.

Mom jobs are this mom's best friend. I have my own rainy day fund to spend however I like, no questions asked. It's like the old saying about living a healthy lifestyle: "May you never know what you prevent."

The Guilt Gene

After dropping Elena off at her piano lesson, I crossed the town park on my way to the library. It was a beautiful spring day and many families were at the playground. One mother was shepherding three toddlers inside for a potty break. The lead child wore a Batman costume. Another mom shadowed her two-year old, gently guiding him away from the slope. "Let's stay away from the water, honey," she said. Everywhere mothers stood guard while their little ones played.

Ah, the super slow motion pace of those days! Just to go to the Shoppette for a gallon of milk required the entire morning. I scheduled the trip after I had fed Elena, changed her, re-supplied the diaper bag, loaded the car, and made three trips back into the house to get things. Sometimes that errand was the big event of my day.

The hours seemed endless. By evening I was exhausted.

"What did you do today?" Paul asked me when he got home from work. "I mean, besides take care of the baby."

I couldn't think of a single thing.

"Nothing adds up," my friend Robin complained.

"It's like shoveling the sidewalk while it's still snowing," Marilyn said.

One day in the commissary, Stephen smelled ripe and Elena was threatening a meltdown. A friendly retiree paused to enjoy the little ones.

"You know," she said to me, "you're going to miss this."

"Not likely," I grumbled.

But I did. I do. She was right.

"The days are long but the years are short." I survived the era of car seats and Cheerios and endless bedtime stories. Stephen eventually started kindergarten. As the children grew, I got my life back. Why, then, this inexplicable sadness as I walked across the playground that afternoon?

It pained me that my dominant memory of those years was how difficult they were and how put upon I was. I didn't remember enjoying Elena and Stephen as babies. Had I appreciated the gift, the blessing, the honor it was to be the caregiver and emotional presence in their precious lives? Did I see the wonder, or was I frazzled and falling to pieces because I could never finish a task?

I was still preoccupied as I collected Elena from her lesson and fixed dinner. While the children cleared the table, I confessed to Paul what was on my mind.

"I was a bad mother when the kids were little."

"Marna," he said, grabbing my shoulders and looking me squarely in the eyes. "Do you ever think you do anything well enough? Trust me, you've raised two gems," he said, nodding towards the kids.

Still not totally convinced that I should take credit, I sniffled, "Must be the guilt gene on overdrive."

"No more talk like that," said Paul. "I mean it."

A little while later he called from the TV room in the basement.

"Come take a look at this." He had unearthed a vintage videotape from 1996. Elena was five and Stephen was one. Camcorders then were as big as suitcases and had to be hoisted on broad shoulders. That's why Paul filmed and I was in the videos. All the reassurance I needed was there in living color.

"'Gain, Mama, 'gain," said the little boy as I tossed the foam ball and he swung the bat but never hit it. Elena, wearing the red princess cape I made her, gave me a guided tour of her castle behind the couch. Stephen and I intently observed the ants on the sidewalk. All three of us ran through the sprinkler and danced to *The Lion King* soundtrack. I was like those mothers at the playground—present and pretty darn good.

Leaving the Parental Orbit

For years, Paul and I have had regular "calendar meetings." We sit next to each other with our planners and cross reference obligations for the upcoming weeks.

"I'll be out in the field Monday through Thursday," he said. "Home late Thursday. Friday is a DONSA, but I will probably go in. Pencil in that TDY next month."

My entries were more mundane. "Tuesday we have physicals scheduled at the clinic. I have a dentist appointment on Wednesday and Elena has piano on Thursday. Don't forget Thursday is also open house at the elementary school. Try to make it if you can."

Then we looked at long-range events. What about a family vacation? Can we do something for a long weekend next month? As the kids have gotten involved in more activities, their expanding commitments—art club, softball, baseball, guitar—filled more space. Still, I thought of my offspring as sub-categories under my control.

So we were surprised when Elena, our 14-year old, appeared at the doorway with the calendar off her bulletin board. "I need to have a meeting, too," she announced.

Paul and I looked at each other. "OK," I said, "pull up a chair."

"We're looking at a good time to go camping this fall. How does two weeks from now sound?" I asked, pointing at the date.

"That weekend's no good for me," she said. "I have plans."

"You have plans?" Paul repeated. "Like what?"

"On Friday I'm babysitting for the Browns. Kirsten's birthday party is Saturday. Then Rachel and I are going out to be townies on Sunday."

"What's a 'townie'?"

"That's when, you know, we just walk around. We go to the park or the library or the bowling alley. Get something to eat. See who's out."

"Sounds a little vague," I said. "Can you be more specific?"

"No."

"We'll see about that." It was the first I'd heard of the babysitting job and the birthday party. Whatever happened to asking permission? "Are you free the following week?" I asked.

"No. There's a poetry slam on Saturday and a house concert on Sunday."

"Excuse me, Princess, is there any weekend you can spend time with us?"

"Mom, camping's boring. Besides, you see me all the time."

That wasn't true. More often, Paul and I drove off in the minivan with just Stephen. Elena was occupied. She was tired from volleyball practice. She had a headache. She wanted to Instant Message her friends. She wanted to retreat behind her MP3 player. "Quit treating me like a baby," she'd yell if we insisted.

"Remember when we just strapped her in the car and took off?" Paul said after she left our scheduling meeting. "None of this negotiating crap."

This crap was tearing me up. She wanted to launch herself out of our orbit and I didn't like it.

"We used to be her whole world," I whined to Paul.

"Not for long," he gently reminded me. "She wouldn't let you walk her to kindergarten. She asked for her own apartment when she was eight, remember?"

Elena's independent streak had forced constant lessons in letting go. With claw marks and white knuckles, I'd let go of overprotectiveness, sleep, control, a clean house, and adult conversations. Because of her, my hair was graying and all my comfortable habits were gone. She's three inches taller than me now, but I still can't let my baby go.

Military

The military subculture has its idiosyncrasies. On post, the traffic stops at 5 p.m. when the flag is lowered. The national anthem plays before movies. Each installation has, predictably, a commissary, hospital, chapel, club, and general's quarters. I've tried to capture the customs, courtesies, and quirks that epitomize this way of life.

Home is Where You Hang Your Family Pictures

Whenever I watch re-runs of the sitcom *Major Dad*, I laugh hysterically, but not because the dialogue is funny. Either the Marines live in better quarters than Army folks do, or Hollywood took serious artistic liberties with the set. Marine Major John MacGillis and family live in a roomy, two-story house with a wrap-around porch. Inside, there are sconces, bay windows, an eat-in kitchen with a chef's island, and a laundry room the size of Connecticut. In my experience, majors with young children don't live in those houses. Empty nesters do.

One of the more obnoxious ironies of military life is that when you have a houseful of active toddlers and live at Fort Lewis, Washington, where it rains for seven months out of the year, you're assigned a tiny townhouse. Once the children leave for college, however, your living arrangement switches to a 5,000 square foot mansion with mother-in-law suite, butler's pantry, wine cellar, and ballroom.

As the colonel's wife said while she gave us a tour of her new gigantic quarters, "I could've used all this room when I was raising six kids."

The grand homes on old Army posts are listed on the National Historic Registry, but most other military neighborhoods are modest. Unlike in civilian life, when you normally improve the quality of living arrangements with each move, the most you can hope for in the Army is that it won't get any worse.

While living in government quarters over the years, I've often asked myself, "What were they thinking?" Where was common sense when they designed family housing with no front yard, backyard, or parking? My theory is that middle-aged bachelors who still lived with their mothers approved the floor plans. As far as they knew, elfkins delivered clean clothes and stocked the refrigerator each night. What did they understand about running a household with little kids?

I believe that the first set of blueprints put together by a kindly architect (father of three) included a garage with a workroom attached, a den off the eat-in kitchen, a linen closet in the hallway, a real laundry room next to the mud room, and a large patio in the fenced-in backyard. Then the bachelors who approve contracts sharpened their red pencils, loosened their ties, and attempted to "improve the bottom line" of the plans.

"A laundry room? Ridiculous!" said the bachelors. "They can put the washer and dryer in the garage. Wait a minute ... a garage? Let's give them a carport with a storage closet instead. No shed. If they want one, they can buy it themselves. The washer and dryer can go in the kitchen, which, incidentally, is way too big.

"Two and a half baths? Hah! They can get by with one. Then we'll add a few square feet to this linen closet and call it another bedroom. We'll re-design the bathroom so they can't open the door without knocking into the toilet. No vanities, shelves, or storage. Do you know how much those cost?

"And look at this back porch. Concrete is pricey!" said the bachelor, as he reduced it to the size of an envelope. "And forget the outdoor lighting. They can just come inside when it gets dark.

"While we're at it, get rid of a couple closets. They can store their stuff under the beds. What is this, a den? Please! What do they think a living room is for? All you need is a place to watch TV. In fact, let's make it a living room/dining room combination."

With that, Mr. Bottom Line bachelor slammed his red pencil down, cracked his knuckles, and felt pretty pleased. The construction, built by the lowest bidder, came in under budget. Nobody believed they could fit so many families in such a small area.

At many duty stations, I cringed at our living conditions. Those dreary bone-colored walls had paint jobs that slopped over light switches and outlets and windowsills. I suspect that one day the original walls will gradually, nail-hole-by-nail-hole, be replaced by spackling compound, which will disintegrate into a big white pile.

The unsightly features included overhead lights that looked like Tupperware bowls glued to the ceiling; bathrooms with urine-yellow tile or mismatched shades of lime green; chipped bathtubs heaved out of their corners by water damage; pipes that howled like London air raid sirens; peeling vinyl floors; kitchen sinks that clogged on an apple peel; warped range hoods, and cockroaches shellacked to the wooden floor.

After the initial shock of seeing the quarters, my mood had nowhere to go but up. Once we moved in our household goods and arranged the furniture, the despair lessened. I put up curtains, hung pictures, and bought area rugs to hide the floors. I displayed the wedding china in the hutch and planted geraniums in the whiskey barrel by the front door. It looked like home.

Still, the living arrangements left something to be desired. Paul listened to my complaints and offered counter arguments.

"These quarters are crappy," I said.

"Yeah, but we don't pay electric or water bills," he said.

"There's no privacy."

"The children walk to school."

"It's too crowded."

"Yeah, but there's always someone around to help you. It's close to work. I come home for lunch. There are lots of kids to play with," he said.

The "Yeah, but's" were powerful. Military neighborhoods were safe, lively, and close-knit. Ultimately, would I remember the leaking radiators, particle board cupboards, and spit-bath faucets, or will I cherish the memories of family dinners, new babies, Christmas mornings, outdoor barbecues, and backyard Easter egg hunts?

Actress Dixie Carter once wrote, "Home is ... my haven in a

callous world, consecrated by the presence of the people I love most, by the intimate history we have shared in it."

We may have shared it within cinderblock walls, but it was our history, and I have the family pictures to prove it.

Commissary Craziness

When Stephen started preschool, the era of dragging cranky toddlers to the commissary ended. I no longer carried bribes to get through the weekly shopping. While Elena and Stephen antagonized each other in the cart, I doled out Cheerios, followed by Gummy Worms, and finally ending with M&Ms. When all else failed, I held boxes of chocolate milk in reserve. This strategy worked until the paper goods aisle where things unraveled fast, and I still had to get through the death march of Frozen Foods. I gladly left that stress test behind me as the children grew.

When Stephen was in first grade, he had a day off from school because of parent/teacher conferences. With some trepidation, I took him to the commissary.

It wasn't Friday, pay day, or even mid-month, but the parking lot was full.

"The retiree factor," I determined, a totally unpredictable phenomenon.

A gentleman and his college-aged daughter walked beside us to the entrance.

"Stay focused," he counseled her. "Be alert. Remember, we're a team. Follow the plan." Noticing my stare, he smiled, "Just a little pep talk before we start." I saw that he carried a master list of staples with many circled.

"We did this when we were stationed in Italy," he said. "It was forty minutes to the nearest commissary."

"That's a good system," I said.

I approached commissary shopping with the mindset of a division logistician. I'm not anal—I just want to get it done quickly and easily. I directed Stephen to the super-sized cart. They looked just like the smaller ones, but they were stored in a different area. The right cart for the job was important, because I didn't want to run out of space in the dairy section. I placed a blue basket in the cart to keep all the fruits and vegetables together.

This commissary didn't provide an aisle guide like many did, so when we moved here I made my own by creeping through the store and noting where items were located. Then I typed a template, copied it, and posted a blank one on the refrigerator. As we ran out of items I wrote them under the correct aisle and trained my family to do the same. I also planned seven to ten menus as part of my grocery shopping preparation.

I've taken plenty of ribbing for my system.

"You are too much," my friend Philomena laughed when she saw me in the produce section armed with a legal-sized clipboard.

"It cuts the shopping time in half," I said. "And I don't forget as many things." I make two major trips to the commissary a month. "I can email this template to you," I offered.

"I'm not that organized. I've got this." She waved her list, which was scribbled on the back of a cable bill.

Stephen snatched my clipboard and pen. "I'm the Manager," he announced. "I'll mark things off." He was eager to boss me around.

"Mom, why do you have pet food on this list? We don't have a dog anymore."

"That's just what's in the store," I said.

"You spelled chicken wrong."

"It's an abbreviation, son. Cross off 'pineapple,'" I said, tossing a can into the cart.

"No, no! I tell you what to get."

"Okay. What's next?"

"Diced tomatoes."

The aisle marker read "Canned Vegetables."

"We're in the right place," I said, scanning the shelves. "Asparagus, corn, peas. No tomatoes." Hmm. Weren't tomatoes a vegetable?

In the next aisle we found them. They were stacked alongside the spaghetti sauce, pizza kits, and pasta. Of course! By genre, not food group.

It dawned on me that they had reorganized the commissary since my last visit. They did this periodically, and it always threw me for a loop. It meant I had to improvise today and schedule a special visit later to draw up a new schematic. Of the many adjustments asked of a military wife, this was a minor one, so I didn't dwell on it.

"Stephen, you pick a cereal," I said in the breakfast aisle. He reached for Fudgy-Cavity Smacks.

"One I'll approve of," I said.

I overheard another mother say to her son, "Brandon, I'm absolutely not buying you anything else with marshmallows in it. Pick something else—brown sugar, chocolate chip, or frosted strawberry."

"*They* have frosted-brown-sugar-chocolate chip," said Stephen. "We never get stuff like that."

"It's not on the list!" I said, accelerating the cart so abruptly it gave him whiplash. Once Stephen learned we only bought things on the list, mysterious entries like "Play Station" and "Double Stuff Oreos" written in first-grade penmanship started showing up.

"What are we looking for, Mr. Manager?" I asked.

"Napkins," he said. Common sense dictated they would be with the paper products. Did I overlook it on the first pass, I wondered? Retracing my steps, I found only paper towels, tissue paper, and toilet paper. No napkins.

"Circle napkins, Stevie. We'll keep looking."

This was going to take some patience and creativity. We discovered potato chips by the frozen pie crusts. Coffee and pepperoni were nowhere to be found. Chicken was situated in three different spots, depending on whether you wanted whole, boneless, or breaded nuggets.

In the second-to-last aisle Stephen shouted, "I see napkins!" They were next to the charcoal and picnic supplies. Why didn't I think of that?

We finally finished and joined the check-out line, which snaked towards the deli. The wait gave me a chance to spy on people and figure out their stories. One fellow walked by with four bags of walnuts and a quart of apple cider vinegar. Was he operating a still somewhere? Another woman had lodged packs of soft drinks around the rim of her cart. Inside the basket was a stack of ground beef and two fifty pound bags of dog food. She obviously shopped in bulk.

"Stephen, you may pick a treat for being such a good manager," I said. He chose two gooey rewards, which I allowed because he had been such enjoyable company. As we walked out to the parking lot, I recalled how I once felt after shopping with toddlers—bleary, short-tempered, knees buckling. Today there was actually a spring in my step.

"We saved 2% with our coupons," Stephen declared after studying the long receipt. "That means we paid 98%. That's not very good, Mom."

I couldn't stop chuckling at his comment as I handed over my 2% savings to the bagger for a tip.

Having a Baby in a Military Hospital

When women get together, sooner or later the conversation turns to birth stories.

Angela, Patty, and I were talking labor and delivery when Angela asked me about my book on Army family life.

"You're going to write about having a baby in a military hospital, aren't you?" she asked.

I've never had a baby in a military hospital. Elena was born in a freestanding birth center in Maryland. I delivered her on a Sunday evening with a mid-wife and a nurse in attendance. That night we drove home.

When I became pregnant again four years later, we were stationed in Florida, two hours from the nearest military base. Stephen was born in the Women's Pavilion at Tallahassee Memorial Hospital. We paid a little extra for a spacious single room with a private bath. Every five minutes some helpful person knocked with a service to offer—lactation consultant, snack lady, photographer, floor nurse. The evening of our son's birth, Paul and I shared a steak dinner by candlelight in the room. Then they wheeled in a rollaway bed so Paul could spend the night.

"A private room!" Angela, mother of four, shouted.

"A steak dinner!" yelled Patty.

"Okay, ladies," I said. "Tell me all about it."

"The maternity ward at Madigan was open-bay," began Angela, who lived in Fort Lewis at the time. "It was an old World War II building."

"World War II?" I said "What year was this?"

"1990! It was no-frills all the way," she said. "There were ten beds and two sinks. They wanted us all to room-in with our babies. With all those women and babies together, no one got any sleep."

"The worst was when everyone was asleep and my baby

started crying," Patty recalled. "That freaked me out."

"The bathrooms were down the hall. At least those were separate stalls," Angela continued. "I was hooked up to an IV, so I had to roll the entire rig to the showers with me."

"If you wanted clean sheets or an ice pack you had to get them yourself," Patty added.

"That sounds awful," I said sympathetically.

"It was definitely coach class," Angela agreed. "At meal times everyone served their own trays off the trolley. Congealed ham and Jell-o Jigglers."

"Did you have any privacy?" I asked.

"There were hospital curtains between the beds."

"When Kate was born," Patty piped in, "Desert Storm was going on. Fort Stewart had converted the maternity wing to surgical suites for casualties. I labored in the hallway on a gurney until it was time to push."

"What were you thinking, having a baby in the middle of a war?" said Angela.

"There were four of us in the recovery room," Patty continued, "and I never saw a nurse. Once I came back from the shower and found a baggie of Tylenol on the nightstand, so I guess someone stopped by."

I shook my head at the stories. The OB care in military clinics used to be called "Cattle Call." There were no individual appointments. All the pregnant women showed up and signed in—first come, first served. When it was time to deliver, the doctor was the on-call physician that day—possibly a total stranger.

"That was the early Nineties," I said to Patty and Angela. "I wonder if it's any different now."

"Oh yes," they both chimed. "By the time I had my second baby at Madigan," Angela said, "they'd opened the new hospital. I had a semi-private room with one roommate. Same at Fort

Benning with the third."

According to friends with more recent experience, "Cattle Calls" were replaced with group in-briefings and personal appointments. Pregnant women who enrolled in Family Practice could see the familiar face of their doctor in the delivery room. Epidurals were offered during labor.

Maternity care in the military has come a long way. I've even heard that some post hospitals serve new parents a steak dinner by candlelight.

Surviving the Well Baby Check-Up

Paul had just returned from a month at the National Training Center in California, so he had a day off, or a DONSA as it's called now: "Day of No Scheduled Activity."

Elena was a feisty 15-month old, and I had arranged a well baby check-up for her that morning. Paul drove us to the clinic parking lot. I thought he was coming in, but he had other plans.

"I'm going running," he said pointing to the jogging trails by the golf course.

"I thought you were coming to the appointment," I protested.

"Nah, you can handle it."

"Don't you want to meet our family doctor?" I said. "He takes care of Elena. He takes care of me, too."

"Um, some other time." He warmed up with a few calf stretches.

He noticed by the way I huffed off with the stroller that I wasn't too pleased. Soon I heard the "clump-clump-clump" of footsteps as Paul caught up with me.

"Okay, I'll go with you," he said. "I'll jog afterwards."

"Thanks," I said. "This way I can show you the ropes in case you ever need to bring her."

We walked into the Family Practice clinic and took our place in the long line. The clinic looked like a crowded bus terminal, as usual. The orange vinyl seats were filled. Newborns cried and the television in the corner blared out headlines.

"Krajeski," I said, when we got to the counter. "My daughter has an appointment."

"They didn't send her records over," the clerk said. "You'll have to get them from the file room."

I reversed the stroller and crossed the hall to the records room. A young woman was frantically searching banks of color-coded medical charts. Sometimes her quest was successful, other times she just shook her head apologetically.

"This is so annoying," a woman in front of me hissed. "They make you late for your appointment."

Finally, errant records in hand, we returned to the clinic. The line was even longer. Paul shifted from foot to foot, desperately wishing he'd made a clean break when he had the chance.

"Your appointment was at 9:45," said the same receptionist, who showed no sign of recognition. With an exaggerated turn, she looked at the clock behind her: 10:05.

"I know," I said, pleading slightly, "but we had to get her records."

She stamped the chart with a harsh punch and tossed it into a wire basket. "Sit down."

There were no seats. We stood and waited. Elena tried to commando out of her stroller. I knelt down and read her *Go Dog Go* and *Are You My Mother?*

A medic took us into an exam room. She weighed and measured Elena and took her temperature, pulse, and blood pressure. "Any concerns today?" she asked.

"Just a well-baby check up," I said, wondering how badly she needed this. She looked well to me.

"Follow me." We walked down several corridors to a row of chairs. "The doctor will be with you shortly." We waited. Elena ate a few Cheerios. Dad bounced her on his knee. We called grandma on the plastic phone. We played peek-a-boo. I gave her some apple juice.

We finally saw the physician. He and Paul shook hands.

"Is she eating okay? Sleeping fine? Talking? Walking?" the doctor asked as he quickly examined Elena. Except for a nasty diaper rash she was healthy. He scribbled a prescription for cortisone cream.

"Schedule your next check-up on the way out," he said.

The reception room was noisier than ever, and Paul looked haggard. I said I'd call from home for an appointment.

"Down this way to the pharmacy," I pointed. In the center of the hospital, people milled around listlessly. A red sign blinked approximate waiting times. Two hours. Could that be right?

I joined the end of the line marked, "Submit prescriptions here."

We waited.

"Dear, you're in the wrong line," said the kindly Red Cross worker. She directed me to the "Pediatric Prescriptions Only" window.

"Go there and you won't have to wait so long."

I submitted the prescription and waited. Paul walked Elena down the hall. They looked out at a bird's nest. They ate cheese crackers from the vending machine.

Finally, the pharmacist called our number and handed me the coveted white paper bag. I sprinted off in search of my family. Fortunately for me, Paul had kept Elena occupied or I would have been really frazzled.

The three of us walked outside to the car and I buckled the baby in her seat.

"You can go for your run now," I said.

Paul sat down in the driver's seat instead. "I'm hungry." After we'd eaten lunch at home, he kicked off his Nike shoes. Elena climbed into the recliner with him to snuggle.

"I promise," he yawned. "I'll never again ask what you do all day."

The Community of Women

Cathy Franks, wife of General Tommy Franks, said she didn't see much of her husband during his last eight years in the Army.

"What did you do?" Diane Sawyer asked her on *Good Morning America.* "Weren't you lonely?"

"The good thing about Army life is that I had my girlfriends to make the tough times easier," Cathy Franks said.

"But an eight-year girl's night out?" Sawyer pressed. She was still confused, but I understood what Mrs. Franks meant. Depending on other women is a survival tactic that military wives learn early. We take care of each other, and we do it well.

There's a hilarious plaque I've seen that reads: "Three wise women would have asked directions, arrived on time, helped deliver the baby, cleaned the stable, made a casserole, brought practical gifts and there would be peace on earth." An Army wife also knows what to do for her friends.

A tradition of hospitality and outreach characterizes a military neighborhood. On our move-in day, Lisa, who remembered us from a previous assignment, dropped in.

"Let me take Elena and the baby back to my house for a little while," she offered.

Dorothy from down the block arrived at lunch with a plate of ham sandwiches and a pitcher of lemonade.

The next morning, next-door-neighbor Kim showed up on our front porch.

"I knew you hadn't unpacked your kitchen boxes yet," she said, setting a basket of muffins and a pot of coffee on the counter. She invited us over for dinner that night.

This is the give-and-take of goods and services in a military community. There are babysitting exchanges and morning phone calls: "Do you need anything at the commissary? Milk? Cereal? Pick up some stamps? No problem."

If you are going out of town, someone will offer to water your plants and get your mail. She'll take you to the airport and remember to get the phone number where you'll be, just in case.

When you have a baby, women on the block bring dinners over for weeks. They gently lift your other children out of your care for a while. They drop off bags of outgrown Onesies for your newborn.

They help out at other times, too. Once when Paul was gone, I got stressed-out about halfway through the deployment. Liz and Robin sensed it and took action. Robin invited us to a cook-out at her house. The following week Liz and I went to a movie, while her husband watched all the kids so I didn't have to get a babysitter. Their thoughtfulness restored me and stopped my downward spiral.

My mother brushes off these stories of helpfulness.

"That's just what decent people do for each other," she says. Maybe in her day, but it's not so common now. Suburban homes are sealed off from each other. When we lived in a Tennessee subdivision, I only saw my neighbors when they drove past at night and shut the garage door behind them. After three years, I'd never even met the couple across the street.

"I've lived in the same place for six years," agreed my friend Marsha, who lives in Northern Virginia, "and I only know a few people. That's how it is."

In a military neighborhood, I have the opposite problem: it's a fishbowl. All kinds of people are in my business. I overlook the intrusiveness, however, because I appreciate the helpful community. A circle of nurturing women is a powerful network. Some ladies find this fellowship in a church group. Military wives, out of proximity and need, form a similar sisterhood. During thirty years with the Army, Cathy Franks learned that nourishing friendships soothe anxieties, ease loneliness, and reduce stress. Recent medical research proves that supportive confidantes are essential for good health.

So when I hear my kitchen door slam and see Sharon walk in with her mug of tea, I know she wants to unburden from the strain of caring for three young children and her elderly parents. We settle in for some "GT," Girl Talk, the best vitamin there is.

A Formal Declaration

I confess that I adore formals. I really do. I woke up at 4 a.m. to see Prince Charles and Lady Diana's wedding. Before the Academy Awards, I'm glued to the red carpet walk on television. I relish the pomp.

I look forward to the black tie events in military life—occasions to get a manicure, don a long gown, and wear my sparkling shoulder-duster earrings. I enjoy the glamorous vibe: making toasts, seeing friends dressed up, and dancing with that cute guy I married.

It's just a heck of a lot of work preparing for these things.

I. Paul

On any given morning, Paul can get ready in six minutes or less. That includes time to shave, shower, dress, brew the coffee, and let the dog out. When it comes to his formal uniform, however, he takes longer than I do. There are so many bionic parts.

He begins in mid-afternoon by hanging his blues jacket on the closet door. He gets out the Brasso, silver polish, rags, brushes, and dental tools to polish up the decorations. Paul has a tackle box full of accessories and bric-a-brac to assist him in this procedure.

He doesn't notice until he's half-dressed that he can't locate his button studs.

We rummage through every knick-knack drawer and jewelry box in the house searching for them. No studs. I quickly phone a local tux shop.

"Do you have button studs?"

"We do but we're closing in five minutes."

"Stay open! My husband's on his way."

Paul leaps down the stairs two at a time, shirt tails flying. Tires squealing, he roars out of the driveway.

Bob, his XO, calls.

"Does Paul have an extra cummerbund? I can't find mine. I think I loaned it to Scott for his wedding." I check Paul's stash but don't see one.

"Try his cell phone," I say. "He can pick one up at the tux shop while he's there."

Immediately, there's another call. It's one of the company commanders.

"I need a set of jump wings," he says, "and Jones is missing his branch insignia."

Fishing through the odds and ends in the tackle box, I say "We've got several. You're covered."

While Paul puts the finishing touches on his jacket, the phone rings again.

"No problem," I hear him say.

"We have to meet Charlie in the coat room at the club," he says. "I'm bringing my extra infantry cord for him." Pointing to the tackle box he adds, "I'm bringing that just in case."

The cloak room looks like a swap meet. Gentlemen in various states of undress barter to complete their uniforms.

"Bow ties," Paul says. "Get your bow ties here. I've got cords. I've got cummerbunds." Several colleagues rush towards him. Deals are struck, exchanges made: "I see your shoulder board and raise you one captain's rank." Miraculously, everyone finishes, and they file out for cocktail hour, looking very handsome.

"There," says Paul, straightening his jacket one final time. "That wasn't hard at all."

II. Marna

My flow chart for getting ready is so complex that I start early and still run late. First, I arrange my outfit on the bed to make sure it's complete. Putting it together required weeks of begging, borrowing, and shopping. I have a satin stole from Mary, a beaded purse from the consignment store, and necklaces from my next-door neighbor.

I shower and shave my legs. Then I paint my toenails red so they match my manicure and look cute peeping out from under the hem of my dress.

While I wait for the polish to dry, I turn to my hair. I can't just let it air dry flat this time. Following my stylist's directions, I attempt to make it look more "evening." This requires layers of products with names like "cement," "pomade," "mousse," and "stiffener." I dry, tease, back comb, and curl. Finally, I stabilize my creation with polymer-enhanced, ultra-hold hair spray glue.

Now for the cosmetics. How do the starlets get that dewy look, I wonder? This is the day to break out foundation, an application so infrequent that a bottle lasts me years. I carefully dab it on with a sponge, covering the redness, hyper-pigmentation, and dark circles. Then I apply blush, powder, and eye makeup. This is tricky because I want to look dramatic, but not theatrical. When I look too much like Cleopatra, I wipe it off and start over with a lighter touch. More touch-ups, another layer of mascara, and I'm done. My feet are tired and my back aches. But now I'm on to the final stage!

"It all starts with the right undergarments," Oprah likes to say. For this clingy knit dress, I've invested in a shaper, an amazing invention that smoothes out my rolls and makes me look five pounds thinner. "Creative underwear," my sister calls it. I think the term "body cast" is more appropriate. Just like putting on support panty hose, this is an aerobic activity, so I order Paul out of the room.

"No husband should have to witness this," I say, closing the door.

When my breathing returns to normal, I reach for the dress. I slip it on, tuck in tags and loops, tie the sash, and adjust everything. I take a final look in the mirror.

"This is a posture dress," I remind myself, sucking in my tummy and rolling back my shoulders.

After a twirl I go downstairs to brief the babysitter and put the chicken nuggets in the oven. Once Paul and I have posed for pictures, I'm ready to be whisked away in my carriage, or in this case a minivan with gummy bears melted into the carpet.

As we drive off I let out a big sigh. The ordeal of getting ready has exhausted me and the evening hasn't even begun.

"I'm just going to rest a little bit," I say, reclining the seat back. With eyes wide open I nap. "I can't close them or my mascara will smear," I explain. By the time we arrive at the club I've perked up a little bit.

"I'll drop you at the entrance," Paul offers, glancing at my strappy heels.

"That would be nice," I reply, knowing that at the Fort Campbell Officers Club I would have to volksmarch from the parking lot, cross a busy street, and commando up a bluff to the front door.

He pulls up underneath the canopy. I open the car door, and swish out to the curb, quite certain all eyes are on me. I'm ready to take on the world!

"Honey!" It's Paul, stage whispering and pointing hysterically. "You have a raisin stuck to your butt."

The Make-Believe Military

Paul was so proud when the U.S. Army Soldier was chosen to be *Time* magazine's "Person of the Year" in 2003. When I showed him the cover picture, however, he groaned.

"What's wrong?" I asked.

"This soldier holding the rifle has her finger on the trigger. You never do that unless you're firing. It's not safe. The guy next to her," he slapped the cover, "doesn't even have rank insignia on his helmet. Obviously, the Army Public Affairs Office didn't approve this picture."

Welcome to the life of picking apart the media's version of the military. It's nothing new to me. As the daughter of an Air Force pilot, I grew up listening to my dad critique the flying scenes in movies.

"Those sound effects don't go with that aircraft," he'd say. One evening while we were watching television, he turned to me abruptly. "What year does this movie take place?" he asked.

"1944," I said.

"That's ridiculous. That fighter wasn't even fielded until 1961!" He stormed out of the room. If the technical details were wrong, he couldn't take it.

These days when Paul and I view movies with military characters we can't follow the story because we're laughing so hard. Even the dramas become comedies. Most of the discrepancies involve the Army's regulation on uniform and appearance.

"His hair is too long."

"The unit patch is on the wrong shoulder."

"He didn't tuck his bootlaces in."

Worst of all: "His air assault wings are on upside down."

All forms of entertainment are scrutinized. Paul and I once attended a dinner theater production of *The Sound of Music*. During intermission, he studied a photograph of the Baron Von

Trapp character, who wore a decorated Navy uniform.

"He has a U.S. Military Good Conduct medal and a Vietnam Service ribbon," Paul chuckled. "Not bad for an Austrian."

We forgave low-budget civic performances, but movie producers had deep pockets and could afford military consultants. Directors and screenwriters staged outrageous scenarios and over-the-top conspiracy plots. If they created a believable world with authentic details, I granted them artistic license. As a drill sergeant once told me, "Take care of the little things and the big things take care of themselves." Instead, Hollywood makes movies with credibility gaps you could drive a convoy through.

A fan of Nelson DeMille novels, I couldn't wait to see *The General's Daughter* when it came to the theater. DeMille was a lieutenant in Vietnam so his depictions of the military are, for the most part, accurate. Well, this time the motion picture team didn't ask him to fact-check their work. In one of the first scenes, John Travolta's character flashed his military identification card, which listed his rank as "1st sarg." That's not even a correct Army abbreviation.

Then there was a scene at a formal military dinner where the white-gloved waiters lifted the silver serving lids to reveal rack of lamb. In twenty years of Army functions, I've never once had rack of lamb. Herbed chicken breast at the buffet line was the usual fare.

After the dinner, the female captain ("the general's daughter") drove home in an Army Humvee as if it was her personal car. In reality, that's totally illegal, but it made a good scene when she stopped to help the "1st sarg" fix his flat tire. I rolled my eyes in the best traditions of Paul and my dad.

It was the same when we saw the movie *Courage Under Fire* about an Army helicopter crew during Operation Desert Storm. I slapped Paul's arm and hissed critiques.

"The pilot is on the wrong side of the aircraft."

"You can't just throw an auxiliary fuel tank out the cargo door like that. It's too big."

"That's not the way a helicopter crashes."

"Look at that armored formation," he added. "They're way too close together."

When *E-Ring*, the television series about the Pentagon premiered, we hoped for an accurate portrayal of the Army. Instead, the standard stogie-chomping colonel appeared in his Class A uniform.

"He's got four ribbons on each row and you're only supposed to have three," Paul noticed immediately. "That mustache isn't regulation. He needs a haircut."

When the character mentioned he'd served five years in Vietnam, Paul quickly calculated, "He's past his mandatory retirement age!"

"Change the channel," I said, handing him the remote. He turned it off instead.

Major Major

I love when someone's name and occupation fit perfectly. My first sailing instructor was Mr. Windus; Elena's orthodontist was Dr. Allbright, and I recently bought perennials from Mrs. Gardiner. I knew of a city planner named Jim Urban and a map-maker named Mr. Flatness. In contrast, I've also read of an attorney named Phibb, a congressional candidate named Lawless, and a surgeon named Dr. Rambo. I sure wouldn't want to be a patient on his operating table.

The traditional address of military rank and name creates funny combinations, particularly if you're a private, major, or general. I'll never forget trying to keep a straight face when Captain Nutt pinned on her oak leaf and became Major Nutt.

In *Together*, a memoir of her years as a military wife, Katharine Marshall related a funny story about her husband, General George C. Marshall. During World War II, Congress created a five-star rank, the equivalent of a European Field Marshal. Although it meant a promotion for her husband, he opposed it. He didn't want to be known as "Marshal Marshall." He was eventually awarded the rank, but his title remained "General Marshall."

Just like my sailing instructor and Elena's orthodontist, some soldiers have the right name for the job. Who better than Chaplain Hart to spread the gospel message of love and forgiveness? There was also a Chaplain Meek, who was destined to inherit the earth. Once I met Private Love who was, of all things, a chaplain's assistant. He and his buddy, Private Eye, couldn't wait to get promoted because they were sick of all the smart comments. You just can't make this stuff up.

When we lived at Fort Leavenworth the majors shared the same housing area. Everyone had a standard nameplate by the front door: rank and last name. Paul and I giggled our way through evening walks. We noticed Major Payne, Major Mann, and Major Minor. And, yes, in the adjacent neighborhood there was a Sergeant Major.

In a happy coincidence, Major Luck and Major Fortune lived close to each other. That cul-de-sac must be prosperous. Major Goodman and Major Goodhart could be heroes in a cartoon, like "Dudley Do-Right." Major Burden, Major Shirker, and Major Hazard don't have it so easy. In fact, Major Hazard was illegal on most interstate highways.

Since soldiers wear their credentials on their uniform, we hoped Major Badges fared well in that competition.

"Major Scout," Paul said. "He must be a cavalryman. Do you suppose Bird and Seagull are aviators?"

"Wouldn't it be funny if Major Outlaw were a military police officer?" I commented. "He might become General Outlaw." Even in renegade military circles that wasn't a good thing. Rules and regulations were very important in the service.

No doubt, Major Battle's unit was filled with thrill seekers. Anybody with the last name of Steele, as in "nerves of," automatically became a fast tracker for promotion. I recently saw an Air Force officer on television named General Jumper. I thought, "Sir, you should be a paratrooper with the Army's 82nd Airborne Division." What a shame to waste that name on a fighter pilot.

Major Thrasher and Major Tiger sounded harmful to life and limb, but they were killer names for warriors. Bosses such as Major Tasker and Major Savage might create tense workplaces. It was a Major Riske that kept you on Major Edge. I wondered if Major Fear did that, too.

"The only thing to fear is Fear himself," answered one of his subordinates.

Major Powers had a poetic name for a soldier. If he shined on promotion boards, he'd eventually become General Powers, which sounded like something granted only by Congress.

There was never a Marshal Marshall, but we had a Major Major. If we didn't have these great names to provide us with private laughs through the years, we'd all be in a General Funk, don't you think?

The Imperial Officer's Wife

Back when I was a lieutenant in the Army in 1987, I over-heard a colonel say to a captain, "I'd like to give you a company command in my battalion, but it's too much work for a single guy. I've got to give it to someone who's married." The understanding was that the wife would do some work, unofficially, of course.

The role of the Army wife is ambiguous at best. We operate in a social hierarchy that's strongly implied but never stated. Right now, hamstrung between traditional Army expectations and modern ideals, it's doubly tricky. Most of the conflicts I've witnessed erupted when contemporary attitudes confronted old school pressures.

We've all encountered the Imperial Officer's Wife (IOW)— that woman who wears her husband's rank. She likes to order other wives around, which never works out very well.

No one compared to Mrs. X. After her husband took command, she hosted the first coffee. Normally, this was when the leader would say, "New year, new group of ladies. What do we want to do?" Instead, she stepped up to her bully pulpit.

"All of the coffees will be at my house. They'll start at six and last exactly one hour. I'll choose the guest speaker. We're not going to discuss this. It's just the way it's going to be."

When she finished, the silence was deafening, all the air left the room, and the gathering quickly dispersed. On the way to our cars I heard more than one woman say, "If that's the way it's going to be, I'm not coming back." They didn't. In subsequent months, it was a good turn-out if four people came to the coffee.

Eventually, the monthly meetings moved from Mrs. X's house to the battalion conference room, an impersonal place with fluorescent lights and plastic chairs. I helped host one with great effort. It was difficult hauling in everything we needed.

"Let's talk about getting together in homes," I suggested to

Mrs. X. "We're women. We like to see each other's houses."

"You just want to show off yours," said Mrs. X.

Nevertheless, she brought it up. We discussed the topic at length with other ladies, and everybody who spoke agreed they'd prefer someone's living room.

"Well, let's just keep it here for now," concluded Mrs. X.

"Then why did we even talk about it?" asked one wife under her breath.

Frustrated, I asked an older friend for advice.

"Bite your tongue until it bleeds," she counseled. "That's a very useful thing to learn in this business."

I bit it until the year ended and Paul got assigned to another unit. Mrs. X's stab at a farewell luncheon for me and two other women was to meet us at the PX food court. As we ate, Mrs. X kept scanning over my shoulder to see if anyone more important had arrived.

"Marna," she said distractedly, "I'm sorry that I didn't get to know you better. My philosophy is that you just do what you're told to do. That's what I had to do, and everything turned out fine."

My head flamed. I was tired of confrontations with Mrs. X, so I bit my tongue again. But if I had spoken, this is what I would have said:

"Here's a new philosophy to consider, Mrs. X. 'Power with, not power over.' You can issue orders all you want, but wives don't have to obey them. We're not troops. We're civilians and volunteers. Our hope is to build a team so we can socialize and look after each other. Women want to be a part of that, but it's always a choice, so we have to make it worthwhile."

Instead, I choked down my macaroni and cheese and went home.

Unfortunately, my good buddy Tara soon joined Mrs. X's coffee group.

"Don't say a word to Tara," my older friend advised. I never would have volunteered the information, but Tara brought it up.

"How does Mrs. X operate?" she asked.

"It's her way or the highway," I answered.

"Thanks for the warning," she said.

It wasn't easy to wear out sweet and gracious Tara, but the IOW succeeded.

"I sure hope people come to her farewell coffee," Tara grumbled after a year. "I don't know a single woman who likes her."

IOW's like Mrs. X cycle out, and good riddance. On the other hand, there are commander's wives like Lynda Zais, who always solicited input from the younger wives. She was very kind when I had my first baby, sending gifts and calling often to check on me.

"That lady has a lot of heart," said my father after he met her. Lynda and I still exchange Christmas cards. The payoff was a decade and a half of friendship and mutual respect. As for Mrs. X, I can't even remember her last name.

Order of the Artichoke Dip

I once watched Martha Stewart demonstrate how to make quesadillas for a party appetizer. Standing before a hot range with the skillet splattering oil all over her, she explained how simple it was. Chop, grate, fry, slice, and let the production assistants clean up the greasy mess later.

A complex project like that right before a party is a fantasy, Martha. I'm still scrubbing the commode in my slip when the guests arrive.

Thanks to the lifestyle industry, the road to entertaining is paved with unrealistic expectations. The media-fed images tell me dinner parties should have themed decorations, elaborate buffets, matching china, and breathtaking desserts. In fact, the vignettes in my Williams-Sonoma book were created by a platoon of chefs, stylists, designers, and photographers. If I thought I had to duplicate the event single-handedly I'd be too intimidated to begin. Either that or I'd have one major dinner a year that would be such a chore I'd hate Paul and all the guests on arrival. In any case, I'd deprive myself of the pleasures of fellowship.

Socializing over food is one of my favorite traditions in the military culture. I love getting together with friends, and we do it a lot. It's taken me a long time to achieve competence as a hostess, I confess. Along the way, I've had some spectacular flameouts.

I once made pork roast that turned out gristly and tough. It was either a bad cut, or I prepared it wrong. I'm not sure which, but it was an unqualified disaster. Another evening, I served chowder which tasted like wallpaper paste. Paul brought the salt shaker to the table and all my guests shook generous amounts into their soup. I had also scorched the grilled sandwiches. Unfortunately, I had no back-up plan, so I scraped off the charred parts, cut the sandwiches into wedges, and served them burned-side down.

Through my embarrassments I learned important lessons.

The most important one was to lower my standards. There's no shame in simplicity. Entertaining is not a competitive sport, with each of us trying to outdo one another. When I took my ego out of the picture the perfectionism left, too. The intent is to relax with friends.

I plan small scale get-togethers. A few friends and I have coffee and pastries on the front porch, or some families come over on a Friday evening. Finger foods, rather than sit-down dinners, work well. Not everything has to be all-out. I have long suspected that all I really needed to have on hand was cold beer and plenty of artichoke dip.

We eat, but it's not about the food. It's an opportunity for unstructured conversation and socializing. In a moment of culinary elitism I once agreed with a friend who said, "If the recipe calls for cream of chicken soup, it's not cooking." Now I realize how arrogant that was. It doesn't matter if it's chicken soup or chicken chow mein take-out, when the company is right, you can't go wrong.

Grocery Store Envy

Every once in a while, I dress up and make a special trip to an upscale civilian grocery store. This usually involves an hour drive to the nearest large city, like Nashville or Kansas City, but it's worth it.

These elegant places are a far cry from our beloved commissary. Except for a jar of artichoke and caper relish, I don't buy anything. Visiting them is an escapist fantasy for me. I'd shop there if we had blue chip portfolios and read the *New York Times* every Sunday at our country home.

When I walked in to the civilian market, it felt like I was entering a four-star hotel. Jazz played in the background, the chandeliers looked like cast-offs from the Waldorf-Astoria. Next to the customer service desk, there was a children's playroom. My son was at preschool or I would have left him with the grandmotherly attendant. I still had post-traumatic stress from our last payday trip to the commissary. Opposite the playroom, there was a ferny cafe featuring homemade soups, cappuccino, and freshly baked bagels.

This was an exhausted mother's dream. I could do all my errands in one place. There was a bank, pharmacy, UPS counter, and dry cleaner. The place was a commissary, PX, Shoppette and a liquor store all in one! They even had their very own cigar humidor.

I wandered by a large display of prepared foods. There was "Take and Bake" of stuffed peppers, fettuccini Alfredo, creamed spinach, twice-baked potatoes, Southwest chicken, fresh guacamole, and au gratin potatoes. Whole chickens turned on an open spit. Polite help in snowy-white aprons offered samples of chocolate mousse, which I gladly accepted.

The deli was unlike any I'd ever seen. Besides the standard ham, roast beef, and macaroni salad, there was citrus orzo, panini grilled to order, artichoke dip, and roasted pepper salad. The meat department sold Greek seasoned chicken kabobs and stuffed Cornish game hens. Everywhere I looked there was an easy answer to the age-old question, "What's for dinner?" If I ever won the lottery I could afford this answer. Did I mention this was a fantasy?

As for produce, we who shop exclusively in the commissary lead a sheltered life. There's a vast world out there beyond iceberg lettuce: kohlrabi, eggplant, star fruit, bok choy, kumquats, arugula, chard, and at least six different kinds of peppers. Besides the standard white button mushrooms, there are shiitake, oyster, and portabella. The tomatoes alone made the trip worthwhile. I hadn't seen a ripe one since I started shopping at the commissary.

"Theatrical" was the only word to describe the seafood department. Weathered lobster traps were mounted on the seascape mural. Fisherman's boots leaned against a sun-faded buoy. I could almost hear honking gulls and crashing waves. Wait, they'd actually piped in sound effects. Was that sea spray on my face?

The "IMAX" experience aside, our military pay wouldn't go far at this upscale market. Blinking digital shelf tags told me all I needed to know. I noticed the pesto cost twice as much here as at the commissary.

In exchange for the big savings at the checkout, I've accepted the commissary's utilitarian atmosphere and limited selection. Besides, Elena and Stephen don't share my love of shrimp and watercress. They think eating a chili dog is a sublime experience.

Shopping at four-star stores isn't realistic now, but prowling the aisles still thrills me. When I'm an old lady living with my cats, I'll shop here exclusively. Then I'll slink home with my brioche and hunks of Stilton and enjoy every delicious bite.

Me

In the 21st century, few women define themselves solely by their home and family. Military wives also desire fulfilling work that provides socialization, stimulation, and structure. A career is difficult, however, because of the frequent relocations. Also, despite some changes in the military mindset, the pressures to be a conventional wife, volunteer, and hostess linger. How does a modern woman maintain her identity while dealing with the expectations and demands of life in the service?

A Very Cedar Christmas Tree

It was my first year out of college, the first year in my own apartment. I was a second lieutenant attending flight school at Fort Rucker, Alabama, and Christmas approached.

My roommate and I wanted to decorate our small, pathetically bare apartment with a real tree. I saw a notice in an advertising circular that read, "Cut your own cedar Christmas tree: $3." The price appealed to my Midwestern thrift, and the "cut your own" satisfied my work ethic.

I wasn't sure what a cedar tree looked like, but my flying instructor reassured me.

"It's the kind we always had when I was a youngster in Virginia," he said.

One Sunday afternoon my roommate and I borrowed a hacksaw from the landlord and set out to find a tree. Our challenge was to pick one small enough to fit in the back of her Honda Civic.

It was dusk when we finally arrived at the rural property. The owner led us toward the woods. Only the sound of feet trampling dry leaves disturbed the silent December afternoon. It was so quiet that a few sheep drifted out from behind the brush to peer at us.

Cutting our own tree was folksy and rustic—far better than browsing the rows of trees in a supermarket parking lot. We carefully eyeballed the chosen tree to make sure it would fit into the hatchback, but our calculations were way off. The trunk was too long to fit, even after we sawed it down. Fortunately, the farmer gave us some twine and we tied the back door closed the best we could. Then we bumped off down the dirt road.

We made one stop at a variety store to buy some trimmings. In keeping with the simple beauty of the tree, I knew exactly what decorations I wanted. It wasn't a lush evergreen, but it had charm. We set it up in front of our living room window so the neighbors—fellow flight students—could enjoy it as well. Then we decorated it with tiny white lights, red bows, and baby's breath. It was lovely.

"Reminds me of *The Walton's Family Christmas*," said my roommate.

The tree brightened our drab little apartment so much that we kept it up until the evening we departed for leave. Flight school recessed for two weeks and we, like most of our friends, were hastily packing to get out of town. With the daily tension of classes fading, holiday spirit rushed in. The weather even cooperated. Although it was southern Alabama, there was a wintry nip in the night air.

Several friends in our flight class stopped over for some "Christmas cheer" on our last night together. We played carols and toasted the season. Then, after the last holiday wish was exchanged, we turned to our Christmas tree. We removed the makeshift ornaments and dragged it out past the wood line in the back. The next morning we shut the door to our apartment and didn't return until January.

Since then, I've had much grander Christmas trees, but my three dollar cedar tree with the red bows taught me what comfort there is in tradition when one is far from home and family.

Bring on the Beige Life

All my life I've been a military family member, except when I was on active duty myself. My scrapbooks show a series of expired military ID cards; first a beige one with the face of a teenage Air Force brat, then a green one after I was commissioned an Army lieutenant.

During my five years on active duty I married Paul, who was also a service member. When I got out of the Army in 1990, I once again carried a beige ID card. Becoming an Army family member after being an Army captain had its, what you might call, "disempowering" moments.

The day my time on active duty ended, Paul and I went to get my new ID card. When the clerk called our name, we both followed her to the desk.

"The sponsor only!" she snapped. Pointing at me, she said, "Sit in the waiting area." I retreated to the orange vinyl furniture and months-old copies of *Field and Stream.*

Only the day before, the clerk who rudely directed me to my seat would have addressed me as "Ma'am" and saluted me outside. Today, I couldn't even make my own name board for the photograph. My sponsor did that. Did they take me for a functional illiterate?

Kathi, a friend who was a Department of the Army civilian in Germany, found her status drastically reduced after her wedding to a soldier. She was issued a new ID card which listed her husband as the official sponsor. When she surrendered her old card, she relinquished many privileges she had come to expect.

"I couldn't even put something on lay-away at the PX without Tom's signature," Kathi recalled. "My housing allowance and gas ration cards were discontinued." This happened despite the fact that she continued in the exact same job.

I have also felt frustrated with my civilian standing. If I had the old rank on my shoulder, I'm sure the assistant at the immunization clinic wouldn't have informed me so testily to bring my daughter's shot record next time. I yearn for rank as I wait in the long line at the pharmacy or commissary, just beneath the sign that reads, "Military in uniform have priority."

And there's always payday, the time I am reminded by the absence of a paycheck that we are now a one-income family.

I was rifling through my wallet and saw a card with an unfamiliar number on it. On second glance I realized it was my own Social Security number. It had been so long since I needed it that I didn't even recognize it. I can recite my husband's number on demand, but have to look through files to confirm my own.

Sometimes, with a generous dose of humor, I compare my past and present roles. I used to be concerned with training schedules and property books. Now I wonder about the best times to shop at the PX and what laundry soap to buy.

In the final appraisal, I regard my beige ID card with fondness and gratitude. Because of my new status, I was able to stay home with Elena and Stephen. That job had immeasurable perks and rewards.

Don't Call Me Dependent

I once attended a baby shower for a friend in Kansas. She was on active duty, as were several of the other women with us at the restaurant. During lunch, someone at the table used the word "dependent" during the conversation.

"I think the official term is 'family member' these days," I said.

"Oh," said one of the wives. "I grew up an Army brat so I don't mind being called a 'dependent.'" This was from someone who had graduated from West Point and served five years in the military!

I'll say right up front that I have a problem with it. Replacing "dependent" with "family member" was one of the most enlightened things the Department of Defense ever did. "Dependent" is insulting. As an Army wife I need to be resilient, strong, and independent. That archaic word is a relic that doesn't belong in our contemporary vocabulary.

Old habits die hard, however, so I still hear it. "We're having a 'Dependents Cruise' this weekend," said our Coast Guard friend as he announced the annual afternoon boat ride for husbands, wives, and children.

"Is that what it's called—a 'Dependents' Cruise?'" I asked incredulously.

"Yeah. Why?"

"It's just that they usually say, 'family member' these days," I said.

He rolled his eyes. I could tell he thought my comment was stupid.

"I don't see what's wrong with the word 'dependent,'" he replied. "You're dependent on the sponsor for your military benefits."

"Then call us 'sponsorees,'" I said. "Just because we've always done it a certain way is no reason to continue the practice."

The military outgrows designations all the time: "dog tags" became "identification tags," "mess halls" are now "dining facilities," and "pay stubs" are Leave and Earnings Statements. Several years ago, the command at Fort Campbell announced that Family Support Groups would henceforth be known as Family Readiness Groups. They thought the name change encouraged spouses to actively anticipate deployments by educating themselves on phone trees, chains-of-concern, and checklists. It also recognized that Rear Detachment duties were integrated into the mission posture of the unit.

"'Dependent' isn't meant to be a slur," say those who believe the conversation is trivial. I admit it's become something of a campaign for me, but the reasons go beyond spin, semantics, or political correctness.

I'm fascinated with words. They carry powerful associations. For instance, even though it began as the name of a country in Southeast Asia, "Vietnam" now vibrates with strong emotional, historical, and political meanings. In the same way, "Chappaquidick" prompts a host of responses, and few people know it's actually an island off Martha's Vineyard.

A dramatic lesson in the implied sense of words happened while we were stationed at West Point. At the military academy, the chair of the Physical Education Department wears the title "Master of the Sword." When he announced his retirement, a female colonel was offered the job. The only problem was what to call her. Certainly they couldn't use a "Mistress," with its bodice-ripping connotations. "Madame of the Sword" sounded like someone running a bordello. They finally elected to keep "Master," citing its definition as "an expert," rather than a masculine form of address.

These examples show that words are freighted with baggage. What's less obvious is their power to influence perceptions and shape identity. We must choose them carefully. To show how enlightened we've become, it's time to consign "dependent" to the museum archives. Call me a family member, an Army wife, a spouse, a soccer mom, "the missus," or Household 6. Just don't call me a "dependent."

Secret Society of Margarets

My new neighbor Meg recently stopped by for a visit.

"Are you a Margaret?" I asked, as I poured her coffee.

"Yes," she said.

"That's my name, too."

Later that week, a mother arrived to pick up her son at our house. She introduced herself as Peggy.

"Are you a Margaret?" I said.

"I am."

Another woman down the street confessed, "My real name is Margaret Mary, but everyone calls me Molly."

Meg, Marna, Peggy, Maggie, Molly, Marge, Margo, even my mother's childhood friend, Mugs. We're all members of the Secret Society of Margarets. Like subversives, we're embedded in this culture.

I was christened Margaret Edwards Ashburn, a very English designation which sounded, someone said, as if I should be writing sonnets. It has special ancestral ties. I was named after my great-grandmother on my father's side, Margaret Edwards.

Few Margarets go by their given names. Because of its quantity of letters (almost one quarter of the alphabet!) or its pleasing diversity of vowels and consonants, Margaret lends itself to many permutations. "The variants and diminutives of Margaret are seemingly endless, but modern usage embraces them all," reports a baby name book I consulted. The author listed a paragraph of nicknames, including some I'd never heard of: Greta, Gretchen, Rita, Madge, and Gert.

Since it's familiar and easily remembered, I usually introduce myself as Margaret. Invariably, as folks get to know me, they'll say "You don't seem like a Margaret." I guess it conjures up a blue-haired spinster who keeps company with Mable, Evelyn, and Gertrude at the church sewing circle. Personally, I think it's a fine traditional name, but modern parents are enamored with happening names like Becca and Madison.

So I'll say, "You can call me Marna if you want." Since it's a much less common nickname, the transition is easier if we start with Margaret, sort of like training wheels. Then people don't misunderstand and call me Marva, Mona, Marina, Monica, or Marla.

"Marna," they ponder for a moment. "That's interesting. How did you get that?" I blame it on the dubious linguistic development of an older sibling. My sister was a toddler when I was born and she couldn't say, "Margaret." It came out "Marna." So that's how my parents referred to me.

"But where did the 'N' come from?" friends persist. Who can say? Nicknames have a long precedent of maverick letters. How did we get Bill from William or Chuck from Charles? There's no rhyme or reason.

To most, "Marna" is an agreeable moniker, except to my uncle, a Southern gentleman of a certain age.

"I'm still calling you Margaret, no matter what," he posited.

"That's fine," I said. To me it's like the difference between Dave and David. I answer to either. Once a Margaret, always a Margaret, even if she's in a Secret Society.

Cooking School

The spring sunshine was delightfully warm as I climbed into Robin's red van. She, Anita, and I were driving to Nashville to attend the *Southern Living* Cooking Show. The morning demonstration was to be held at the Opryland Hotel, followed by a luncheon featuring all the recipes.

Paul stood on the curb, joking with us as we were about to leave.

"I hope they teach you how to make Polish sausage," he said, "and bratwurst," knowing I avoided everything in the wiener family. "Seriously, enjoy yourself," he said. "Don't worry about anything."

He had just returned from a month of training in California and the battalion had three days off. He looked forward to puttering in the garage and playing with Elena and Stephen when they got home from school. I was happy to have Paul back but I also needed a break with the girls. It was a welcome change from the survival mode of the previous four weeks.

Freed from household demands, I relaxed with my buddies on the drive down I-24. My children were in the capable hands of their father, not a babysitter, which meant I didn't have to race back to meet the bus. Paul had let me sleep in that morning while he fixed their lunches and got them off to school.

His simple gesture meant so much. What a relief to have an extra set of hands around the house again. With a big sigh I sank into the minivan seat.

"No wonder I'm so dogged out," I said, more to myself than the other two. "Parenting is a two-person job and I've been doing it all myself."

There was an awkward quiet in the car. Clearly, I'd said something wrong. I glanced around uncomfortably. Military wives don't confess that they're exhausted. We're supposed to be capable and in control at all times. I'd broken the code, mentioned the unmentionable. Anita glared at me.

I braced myself for a tongue lashing like the one I'd overheard at a coffee.

"You're obviously not a good military wife," said one woman to another, "or you could handle this stress better."

Instead, Robin, the energetic mother of two girls, looked at me in the rearview mirror.

"Yes," she said softly.

Her response spoke volumes to me. "Yes," she meant, "parenting alone *is* hard work." Yes, she's tired and frazzled, too. She knew exactly what I meant. The tension in the van disappeared.

"It's good that we're talking about it," commented Anita, another dynamo who seemed to chair every committee at school.

For the first time, the three of us confided openly. I needed to know that I was not the only one who felt tired, pressured, or overwhelmed. If it looked like everyone else had the world by the tail while I floundered, I hesitated to speak up, even when I needed a conversation just to vent.

"Why bitch?" said a friend when I asked how she was holding up while her husband was in Korea. "No one wants to hear it anyway."

I didn't mean bitching; I meant sharing. The pressure to be stoic and chin-up has long been a part of the military wives' code. "She needs to quit whining and SUCK IT UP!" screamed a woman in an email about another wife. "I've had it SO MUCH WORSE!" Where does this attitude get us? Stressed out and on anti-depressants.

A few years ago, the Army Center for Health Promotion produced a deck of cards imprinted with wellness tips. The Queen of Clubs counseled, "Help each other when things are tough." If we took her advice and joined together instead of judging each other, we'd all cope better.

At the *Southern Living* school, Robin, Anita, and I watched a chef prepare crab cakes, spinach soufflé, and Key Lime pie. We also cooked up a conspiracy of our own on the drive down. From then on we'd have more compassion and less competition; more openness and less edge. The Queen of Clubs ordered it.

Craft Corner

"I spin my wheels and collect unfinished projects."

I laughed when I read that line in a friend's Christmas letter. As Paul will confirm, I'm also the Queen of Half-Started Crafts. We recently paraded out the annual "Lotsa Ornaments Kit" from the decorations box. The project, which I bought in 1990, contained raw material for 50 felt ornaments. Every evening after dinner I planned to stitch away at my candy canes, sleighs, and snowmen to get in the holiday spirit.

"I'll make an Advent calendar out of them!" I declared. There would be no end to their charming uses.

Since then I've finished fifteen. That's an average of one per year.

I didn't realize how difficult they'd be. Cutting out the meticulous patterns, not to mention embroidering miniature faces and attaching sequins, took a lot of time. All that work for a schlocky elf.

"In another 35 years, I'll have this project done!" I told Paul.

"When the kids are gone you'll finish it," he said.

Before Paul put a stop to it, almost every corner of our house was populated with my trademark works-in-progress.

For a while, it was cross stitch. Every day while Elena took her afternoon nap, I watched *General Hospital* and crafted. I stitched red and green tartan cuffs for our taffeta stockings. For my father, I back-stitched a poem about his home state of Virginia, and my sister got a framed house blessing. Swept away by my enthusiasm, I soon bought patterns for a bell pull and a pillow with my college seal on it. Packets of floss peaked out underneath the couch and coffee table. The pile of instructions, books, Aida cloth, needles, and scissors threatened to take over the living room.

"What can we do about this, Marna?" Paul said.

"The craft store has a cute accessory bag with pockets for all the equipment," I said, "but I didn't buy it because it was so expensive."

"Go get it," Paul said. "I don't care how much it costs."

Around the corner in the laundry room was my sewing nook. The machine, serger, thread, zippers, buttons, patterns, and fabric collection took up a lot of space. This was also a shrine to abandoned ideas. Folded on the table was a summer dress I tried to alter. Fall was nearly over. Underneath the table, there was material for a maternity dress. That baby was in high school now.

"Can I ask you something," Paul said, as he made a futile attempt to tidy the area. "How much fabric does one person need?"

"Believe me, it's nothing compared to other women in my family," I said. My mom has entire rooms in her basement devoted to bolt ends. Laura, my younger sister, maintains several closets full. In the she-who-dies-with-the-most-fabric contest, I wasn't even a contender.

"Besides," I said, "consider how much money I've saved by making curtains all these years."

I felt so persecuted that I retreated to my knitting to calm down. My needles were stuck in the only thing I ever make—a scarf. To date, I have completed approximately thirty scarves, but have yet to progress to anything more complicated. A cable sweater wasn't my goal; I just enjoyed the peaceful escapism of knit two, purl two.

Perhaps, as a stay-at-home-mother, I had an abundance of creative energy on my hands. The daily grind of laundry-cooking-cleaning was process, not product. In my domestic haze, even a misshapen muffler counted as an accomplishment.

Knowing my habits, friends hip to the latest craft fad have often asked if I wanted to start something new.

"You should take up smocking," my mother-in-law said.

"Try stamping. It's so much fun," said Kathleen. "You can

make your own greeting cards!"

"Join my quilting class," Sheila suggested.

I was standing outside when a woman rolled by with a foot locker on wheels. "What's that?" I asked.

"Crop hopping," she said. "Want to come to my home party?"

Scrapbooking. I'm grateful that the trend has made supplies easier to find. I now put all my photographs in acid free books, and they don't fade. But if you ask me, scrapbooking is just another way we women put pressure on ourselves. With the die cuts, lettering, borders, and embellishments, a two-page spread takes half a day to complete. All I've ever done is glue prints in an album and caption them and I'm still years behind. There's a box of pictures under the buffet and one next to the armchair in the living room.

Paul will pass out if I take over another corner with a hobby. Besides, crop hoppers admit it has to be the main extracurricular activity, and that means there'd be no time for sewing, knitting, and cross stitch.

A Patchwork Résumé

"[A military wife] will not embarrass her husband with breaches of conduct, she will take the good with the bad, she will recognize her own worth as a wife and partner, and will not get a job selling real estate downtown in a pathetic attempt to declare her independence."

The General's Daughter by Nelson DeMille

Paul and I sat on the front porch with mugs of coffee, sifting through the Sunday paper. He read the Sports section. I circled employment ads in the classifieds.

"What am I going to be when I grow up?" I wondered aloud. We'd finished unpacking and weren't planning another move for at least two years. Both kids were in school all day. It was time for me to find a job.

Flipping through the notices for registered nurses, I said, "I wish I had a medical background. I could get a job anywhere." Two of my sisters are doctors and one is a nurse, but I never had any interest.

"Remember what Bill's wife said about that?" Paul reminded me.

"That's right. She had a Master's degree in nursing, too," I said. She told me it was a tough field for an Army wife. "They offer me the worst shifts because I'm new," she said. "Night shifts were out because Bill was in the field so much and I had to be home for our daughter."

So much for nursing. "How about education? There are always lots of openings for teachers," I said.

Next to me, Paul snorted.

Whenever I volunteered at the school I came home frazzled

and exhausted. I love my own two children passionately, but couldn't deal with a class of active youngsters. "Whatever teachers get paid it's not enough," I told Paul.

Besides, my friend Liz, an educator by degree, hasn't worked in her field for six years. "We move every two years," she pointed out. "I'd have to be certified in every state!"

I sipped coffee while I contemplated the next career option. "Car sales," I said. "Or the bookstore is hiring. I love books."

"Don't do that. You're overqualified."

"Have you looked at my résumé lately? I'm barely qualified to bus tables." With two degrees in English, I'd be well-educated restaurant help, but my recent work experience was non-existent. I had gaps in my résumé large enough to march a battalion through.

"Let's see if there are any openings for Cookie Mom, Peewee soccer coach, or bottle washer," I said. "I know I can do that."

The work history of military wives, if we have one at all, often looks like a patchwork quilt of short-term employment in different cities. Kris, with a degree in business, was a bookkeeper, college financial aid counselor, day care provider, and substitute teacher in different places. When she found two scanners at school, she plugged them into computers. Suddenly, she had a new position: technology director.

Tracy, who studied business in college, was told by a placement agency in a military town that she was "unemployable." She found work in a downtown jewelry shop. Sheila said that her Master's degree in education had been decorating the hallway since graduation, "and that's about it." Amy, a journalist, clerked retail in a housewares shop. "I don't have time to work my way up at a newspaper," she said. "We're only here for ten months."

Since I left the Army in 1990, I've worked as a personal assistant, aerobics teacher, freelance writer, and doctor's receptionist, in addition to being a mother. Although my field is writing, my attempts at applying for those jobs were disheartening.

I once saw an opening for a part-time editor at a local parenting magazine.

"This is perfect for me," I thought, as I dialed the number.

"I'm calling about the job listing," I said to the woman who answered.

"Tell me about your background," she replied.

With a bachelor's in English and several publication credits, I passed the initial screening. She discussed the next step.

"I'll send you a disk with a few articles on it. Edit them and send it back to me," she said. "Give me your address."

I recited it, but when I got to the "West Point, New York" part, there was a lengthy silence.

"West Point?" she repeated. "Are you military?" Gulp. I should have prepared for that.

"My husband is," I said finally. The phone line crackled.

"How long will you be in the area?" she asked. How did I let myself get sucked into these questions?

"At least two more years." That was a safe answer. Even in the civilian workforce people switched jobs that often.

My interviewer politely ended the conversation. I never got the disk in the mail.

"Excuse me? That's illegal!" yelled my friend Kathy when I told her the story. "She can't discriminate against military family members like that."

"What can I do about it now?" I shrugged. Since the same thing had happened once before when I applied to proofread court transcripts, we decided to strategize with our friend Roberta, an attorney.

"When they ask if you're military," Roberta said, "answer 'Does that make any difference as to whether I'm a candidate for the job?'"

"What if it does make a difference?" I said.

"Then politely remind her that, according to Department of Labor hiring regulations, she's not permitted to ask."

"Don't even go into that," Kathy interrupted. "Rent a P.O. box off post. That'll keep the military address from coming up."

I considered these real-world strategies as I scanned the classifieds, but there were no writing positions advertised in the paper that morning.

"I wish I had a portable career like Dental Hygiene or Physical Therapy," I said to Paul. "Then I could get a job anywhere." Instead, I cobbled a piecemeal work history into a lightweight, functional résumé.

I drained my coffee cup. "Here's one thing I haven't considered. There are openings in every city. 'No experience necessary,' it says. 'Excellent pay.'"

"What's that?" said Paul.

"Exotic dancer."

It Takes a Long Time to Grow an Old Friend

Paul's friendship needs are straightforward. He wants pleasant, conscientious people at work, and someone to go running with on the weekends. Other than that, the kids and I keep him happy.

My social architecture is more convoluted. Relationships occupy a central place in my life, and matters of a woman's heart are seldom simple. In military living I've discovered that some people are friendly, but are not my friends. They're team building or playing politics. Others are relationship vampires, sucking the positive energy out of me. Most, however, are good folks; some become forever friends.

Two centuries ago, George Washington wrote:

"Be courteous to all, but intimate with few, and let those few be well tried before you give them your confidence. True friendship is a plant of slow growth, and must undergo and withstand the shocks of adversity before it is entitled to the appellation."

My 20 years with the Army have brought his words to life. I've learned there are flash friends, and there are forever friends. Discerning the difference has been a beautiful torture.

I. Flash Friends

My sister has lived in Indianapolis since elementary school. Laura married her high school sweetheart, and their house is a mile from where we grew up. She's had the same circle of friends for years. About once a month there's a big, clannish romp with parents, in-laws, nieces, and nephews at someone's house after church. Her support network is familiar, steadfast and, I confess, enviable.

Because Paul and I bounce around the country with the

Army, we've forfeited the nearby community of family and long-time friends. Instead, we have good camaraderie and a shared identity with people who know how to bond quickly.

"Situational friends," Angela labeled them. I call them "flash friends."

Flash friends are more than acquaintances, but I've only known them a short time. They may be neighbors, unit wives, playgroup mothers, or co-workers. We've chatted in the commissary, car-pooled to preschool, and served on the same committees. They're decent relationships, but I've learned that an enduring bond doesn't materialize just because our husbands work together or our children are the same ages. This is the undeniable truth: there's no such thing as instant intimacy.

Many times I've thought of someone as a close friend, when she was really only a flash friend. She shouldn't have been honored with deep confidences because the relationship was too young. Without a strong foundation, it was a tinderbox waiting for the spark of a petty offense or misunderstanding. Then it blew up, leaving many hurt feelings in the aftermath.

"I gave myself away too quickly," said my neighbor Amber, describing a similar falling out. The loneliness and the desire to fit in made us eager, perhaps overeager, for friends. We grabbed at quick connections. Everyone was on her best behavior, and it seemed legitimate. But it was a superficial courtship.

Pre-fab or not, it had to do. The clock ticked down to a permanent-change-of-station move. I had a short period to make a life in a place, and I needed other women to help me through the stressful periods.

Time, the requirement for building a forever friendship, is something I don't have. Just when I've made a few promising starts, we leave.

Some flash friendships fade to annual Christmas card lists, or we simply drift apart. Not every one is a keeper. Air Force wife

Ellie Kay notes, "It's all right for some friends to be temporary and the connection can still be real."

If we're lucky enough to be stationed together again, the friendship deepens. The real treat—and it hardly ever happens—is when we get more than two assignments together. Then we develop lasting closeness.

Flash friends can evolve into forever friends, but it takes patience. Forever friendships are built from the ground up with honesty and shared moments. Like diamonds and fine wine, they need years.

II. Forever Friendships

A forever friend feels like family, but without the baggage.

We may be geographically separated for years, but once we're together again, it's as if only an instant has passed. These relationships have survived time, distance, and disaster. They're so cherished it's almost sacred.

A forever friend tells me the truth, not just what I want to hear. She won't sugarcoat it, but she'll only give it to me if I ask. Then she knows I'm ready to listen.

A forever friend has the confidence to say, "Quit being so needy," or "Get over it already." With her years of steadfastness, she's earned the right to comment candidly, even if it sounds harsh.

A forever friendship has withstood the misunderstandings, the temporary alienations, and the "I'm-not-speaking-to-her now's" during the stormy adolescent years of the relationship. Snits and hurt feelings still happen from time to time, but we recover from them quickly. She's seen me be petty, short-tempered, and ill-humored. She accepts me, warts and all, because she also knows the best.

The communication between us is almost telepathic. She can

read the message conveyed by the lift of my eyebrow. We finish each other's sentences. Sometimes I know, just by the ring of the telephone, that she's the one calling. A forever friend shares her hurts, her losses, and her vulnerabilities. She's honest with me as with no one else. We remember each other's birthdays, anniversaries, favorite colors, and soft drinks of choice. She knows I put sweetener in my iced tea but sugar in my coffee.

In my scrapbook I have pictures of her wedding, the christenings of her children, and every Christmas photo from the past decade. I've written her parent's phone number in my address book. If I call her at 3 a.m., she'll say, "What is it? What's wrong?" Her company is as warm and comforting as a mug of hot chocolate on a chilly day.

The more time that passes the tighter the bond becomes, even if we live in different cities or countries. Constancy like that doesn't develop overnight. In our vagabond military life it's tempting to believe that it can. But forever friendship needs a stately, unhurried pace.

I may have a full address book, a platoon of flash friends, and a lively coffee group. Yet I count myself lucky if I have a handful of forever friends in a lifetime.

The Sky Was Blue, Blue, Blue

In 2001, we were stationed at Fort Campbell. Paul had been deployed to Kosovo for six months. I was going to graduate school, taking care of the kids, and managing solo parenthood fine. Then came that awful trauma: September 11, 2001.

———- Original Message ———-
From: Marna
To: Maris
Sent: Thursday, September 11, 2003 7:23 PM
Subject: Marna here

Dear Maris,

Here it is the second anniversary of Sept. 11 and it is bringing back so many memories of that day. I will always remember our walk. You pushing Max in the stroller, him sucking his two middle fingers as usual, happy as can be. When I got home, I felt so good. We had gotten rid of the "brain pudge" as you said, and my mind was clear and I was calm. (That was a very good thing because I often got stressed while Paul was gone.)

The weather that day was gorgeous. It was so sunny and crisp and breezy. The sky was blue, blue, blue. The beauty of that day contributed to my good mood after our walk. I was looking forward to brewing a cup of coffee and chilling out for a few minutes. Then Paul called from Kosovo. He asked me if I was watching the television. I said no. He told me to turn it on; he said the Pentagon had been hit and we were at war.

It was such a nightmare. I remember watching the TV all morning and just being stunned.

I guess I write this to you because you were on the other side of the great divide that day. You and Max were a part of everything that was good and beautiful and perfect about that morning. Of course, I will always remember what I was doing on that day, so you are in my memory for all time. It was just an ordinary walk, but I'll cherish it forever because it stands in such contrast to the loss and horror of that day.

Thinking of you this day (and every day). Hang in there.
Love,
Marna

From: Maris
To: Marna
Sent: Thursday, September 11, 2003 9:17 PM
Subject: RE: Marna here

Dear Marna,
Thanks for the nice letter.

I have been thinking of you a lot lately, and especially today. You are absolutely right, our walk was GREAT. The day was perfect and started out fantastic. When I got home Jim was still trying to sleep, but said to me as soon as I walked in the door, "I guess you have a busy day planned. The phone has been ringing off the hook." I knew I didn't have any plans (as usual) so we listened to the answering machine together and every message was "Oh, can you believe what is happening?!!!!" and "Oh, my gosh, Maris, call me as soon as you can." Jim and I both had a sinking feeling and he said, "Guess we'd better turn the TV on."

WHAT A SIGHT!!! I just sat and cried!!!! And of course being the soldier Jim is he got in the shower and headed to post!!! I felt so alone after he left!!! (He was stuck in traffic for hours!!!)

How our world has changed.

The acts of September 11, 2001 have taken my husband away from us again.

Our family doesn't deserve another year-long separation … But like Jim always says, "Better him to fight this mess then have to send our kids someday."

I wish you were here. I wish we could walk again. This time of the year always brings back good memories of our daily chats. I wish I wasn't always complaining about my aches and pains back then.

I have been walking again, but it isn't the same alone. I guess I am never alone. I always have one kid or the other in tow, but I sure would enjoy your company.

Thanks again for the note.

Friends Forever,

Maris

Daffodils in a Mason Jar and Other Miracles of Spring

Winters can be brutal on me. The short days, sub-zero temperatures, inactivity, cabin fever, extra ten pounds, and pasty skin take a toll on my spirit.

One year, when we lived in New York State, the snow started before Thanksgiving and didn't stop until April. I had a preschooler and a baby and we were on an isolated installation. Some days our only escape from house arrest was to go to the bowling alley for a cheeseburger.

On yet another numbingly gray day I leaned against the window, surveying the frostbitten landscape and the ice-choked Hudson River. It was the time of year that West Point cadets called "The Gloom Period."

"Will this winter ever end?" I moaned, pressing my forehead on the chilly glass.

I was so relieved when warm weather finally arrived. Like a prisoner of war just released from the enemy camp, I fell on the ground and kissed the thawed black soil. Spring was a generous Creator saying to me, "This is your reward for surviving winter."

Watching the natural world soften and emerge after a long, frozen spell is awe-inspiring. My first April somewhere is doubly wonderful because the packed dirt offers up joyful surprises each day. Spring in a new place is a miracle.

Around late March, the earth yawns and rouses itself. Honking geese sail across the sky in a northerly direction. There is light, glorious light. During breakfast—light. For an hour after dinner—light! People emerge, blinking, from their houses. Children ride bicycles and scooters. Where there were snow banks, there are puddles. We wear windbreakers instead of stadium coats.

I greet this fragile truce with winter reverently. The days seem charged with possibility—like that moment when I first learned I was pregnant or the split second at the theater before the curtains open. Bare trees hum and then blur into lizard green. The transformation begins.

Having survived winter's austerity, I'm starved for color. Nature responds with yellow. This is stop-in-your-tracks, no-doubt-about-it, school bus yellow. The mustard buds of forsythia announce the season's parade like a drum major. Drab tangles everywhere blaze into showy buttercup sprays.

Around Fort Campbell the common daffodil grew wild in the spring. They were so pretty and free for the taking. Many times I pulled my car off the road and cut bunches of them from the easements and ditches and hardscrabble places where they grew. I kept a pair of garden scissors in the trunk just for this reason. The rooms in my home were decorated with jars of daffodils.

After winter I'm even well disposed towards dandelions. Their cheerful color pops out in delightful ways. On the way to Stephen's preschool there was a wide, grassy field dotted with dandelions. In the morning light they looked like a constellation of golden stars on a putting green.

I'm thankful for people before me who've left a legacy of flowers. After our first winter at West Point, purple crocuses pressed up through the late snow like petulant preemies, determined to survive. A riot of red tulips emerged, unbidden, in the planting bed outside our front door. They were so vibrant that people stopped their cars to see if they were real.

I find dogwoods the most heartening of all, perhaps because they flower among the maples and poplars. As I hiked in a state park near Fort Campbell, I caught glimpses of dappled white in the bare woods. The bold blossoms seem suspended in mid-air. What did they remind me of? Floating white feathers? No, more like a mini-blizzard, one of those snow globes that I shake and the flakes slowly settle on a Bavarian scene.

Spring re-enchants my life. My heart gets a gentle lift from each new detail.

How could I not be grateful when the main road at Fort Belvoir shimmered with flowering pear trees? It reminded me of Brandenburg lace wafting in the breeze. *Bel voir* means "beautiful to see" in French, and it was certainly true in the spring. Almost every house in our neighborhood had a squat, gnarled tree in the front yard. In March, their branches burst into fluffy white popcorn. Our circle of quarters looked like a cotton candy wonderland.

"Wow!" my daughter said on our walk. "You could have a wedding here." The trees did resemble a pastel row of bridesmaids. I have long shared the season's sights with Elena, who has been a nature lover since she was little.

"Elena, remember when you asked me last week why we go to church?"

"Yes," she said, skeptical even in the fourth grade. "What if there's no God? Then we're praying to nothing."

I turned her around, the two of us slowly taking in the lush, soprano, chiffon, sherbet, sweetness of spring.

"This," I said, "is how I know there's a God."

My Little Black Dress

I never ignore a clearance rack of evening dresses. If there's a great bargain in my size, I'll buy it. The military social season isn't limited to the occasional holiday black-tie event. With at least two formals a year, I cherish those $39.99 mark downs.

After Paul became a field grade officer, we got invited to dressy events more often, which provoked a wardrobe emergency. I needed evening wear. My short little disco dresses from the Eighties looked like, well, short little disco dresses from the Eighties. I went shopping for something more flattering and current.

When I told the sales associate at Ann Taylor that I wanted a simple cocktail dress, she disappeared to the backroom and returned with a sleeveless black velvet sheath. It looked perfect— elegant, classic, not too trendy. With no taffeta or ruffles, I didn't look like a wedding party refugee. Unfortunately, the first size she brought me was a little too tight, so I asked for a larger one.

While I waited, another customer in the fitting room noticed me.

"Wow, that's a great-looking dress," she said. "I want to try one on." While the sales clerk went to get another dress, I zipped into the correct size. As I twirled around in front of the mirror wearing the form-fitting dress, a different woman admired it.

"What a pretty dress," she said. "Can you get me one?" While no doubt calculating the size of her commission, the sales associate happily trotted off for the fourth time. Later, we all stood together at the cash register with our matching gowns and credit cards.

"Am I getting a broker's fee?" I joked. "I sold two dresses back there."

"Let's make sure we don't show up at the same party," the other lady laughed.

Unlike the rack of off-season party dresses, this gown was full price. It was more than I liked to pay, but I prorated the cost over time. With different wraps and sparkly necklaces, I wore the same dress many evenings. No one noticed until my sister, Laura, was browsing through my photo albums.

"Wait a minute." She flipped back a few pages, then forward a few more. "It's the same dress. Yes, look here! You have on the same dress. There," she pointed to the Fort Leavenworth Welcome reception photograph.

"And here," the superintendent's dinner.

"And here," the ten year reunion at West Point.

"And here," the spring formal. "Unbelievable. It's the same dress every time." Elena produced another scrapbook, and they began counting the appearances.

"Ten!" they announced. "You wore that dress ten times."

"Eleven if you count the Christmas party in '98," I said. "The pictures didn't turn out."

"How long did you have it?" Laura asked.

"Five years," I said. "It's in Elena's costume box now." When the seams stretched and the velvet frayed, I retired it.

I resumed perusing clearance racks. Ever the bargain hunter, I was doing a routine shelf check at Goodwill when I came across a full-length black dress for $25. This one had spaghetti straps and a chiffon sash that crossed the bodice and tied in back. The boutique tags were still attached and it was my size. The old velvet sheath was properly replaced.

My friend Angela was going to the same military ball, and I couldn't wait to tell her about my luck. A few days later she phoned me back.

"I found a dress at the church thrift shop," she bragged. "If it doesn't fit, I wasted less than $3."

She looked stunning in her backless purple moiré satin. Not as good as me, of course, but my dress cost ten times more.

I Won't Say Goodbye Now

There are a few lies I often tell myself:

"I'll just run to the commissary for a few things."

"When the kids go back to school in the fall, I'll have a lot more time."

"After this next pay raise, we should be doing okay."

And the biggest whopper of all: "I won't say goodbye now, because I'll see you before you leave."

Goodbye is a four-letter word to me, except it actually has seven letters. I hate it. It's so factual. Goodbye is short for, "Our time together has come to an end, and we may never see each other again."

So I put off saying it. And put it off. And put it off some more until the last possible moment. By then the friend is gone, so there's no chance for a farewell. My technique makes it easier to cope with transitions. It's a gradual adjustment instead of an abrupt rip. As I say, "We'll see you again," it's entirely possible our paths will cross in the future. The Army is a small place. One couple we knew as lieutenants became our next-door neighbors at Fort Leavenworth ten years later. So in the back of my mind that model chugs along: no need to say goodbye when I'm going to see you again within the decade.

Paul and I once attended a going away party for some friends, but nobody was saying goodbye. We nibbled at the nine-layer dip. We compared Caesar salad recipes. We talked and laughed. At the end of the evening, I said, "We'll see you before you leave, so I won't say goodbye yet."

Some call it the coward's way. I see it as survival. Departures are a way of life in the Army, but they're still sad. I'd rather let people drift out of my life. That way I don't have to say Goodbye, with a capital "G"—the tearful one, the one for the record.

Like when my friend Sheila moved to Germany, I saw her off

in a big emotional scene. We were sobbing and hanging on to each other. We'd been together four whole years; that's like 28 years in civilian life. Her husband shook his head as he watched the ordeal. "You guys are killing me," he said. "Why do you do this to yourselves?"

Why indeed? Why not just slink out of town under cover of darkness? It's so much easier. In the weeks before my friend Kathy left I had many opportunities to say goodbye formally. We had a monthly coffee where we gave the ladies who were leaving their gifts. Then there was a unit Hail and Farewell. I sat with her at the school's spring program, and again at the end-of-season baseball banquet. After she took me out to lunch for my birthday, I said, "I won't say goodbye just yet, because I'll see you before you leave."

While denial is a very useful mechanism, ultimately I had to confront her absence. One evening Paul came home to find me keeping company with a two-pound bag of M&M candies.

"What's wrong?" he asked.

I shoved a fistful of chocolates in my mouth.

"Kathy left, and she didn't even say goodbye."

Me

"Me" was the last chapter I wrote. I resisted it. I procrastinated well beyond my usual habits. I didn't want to start writing about me.

"I'm the narrator in every chapter," I said to my editor. "The readers know who I am. Do I really need a chapter on me?"

"Yes," he said.

"This is so difficult!" I wailed.

"Why? Don't you know who you are?" he asked.

Apparently not. In sixteen years of marriage, fifteen of them as a mother, my sense of "me" had atrophied. I've focused all my attention on the little ones, the home, caretaking, moving, and my husband. There was little time to think about me when confronted with two hungry children, a trunk full of groceries, and dinner to cook, all before soccer practice. This was survival, not self-exploration.

My identity was like art and music at the school budget meetings—the first thing axed. Yet I don't think Paul would say his sense of himself deteriorated with marriage and fatherhood. He continued to claim it, while I rarely did.

"I'm going running," he said one afternoon, sticking his head in the family room where I was folding laundry.

"Isn't that funny?" I thought after he'd gone. If I wanted to go for a walk, first I'd make sure that the baby was napping, Elena was at a play date, and dinner was simmering in the crock pot. Then I'd go hat-in-hand to Paul and say, "Would you mind if I went for a walk now?" Then, if no one were inconvenienced by my absence, I'd leave, mindful of returning quickly.

I had many reference points to check with; Paul had one. I negotiated; he announced. Because of my hypersensitivity to other's needs, I became more and more removed from myself.

"Try this exercise," my friend Stephanie, a life coach, suggested. "Write down everything you are—mother, wife, writer, daughter, whatever." I sat down with a smooth piece of white paper before me and began listing how I defined myself. The direct human relationships came first. "Mother, wife, sister, daughter, friend." Then I put "volunteer, writer, yoga student, teacher," along with a few others.

"Now ask yourself," Stephanie said, "if you're none of these things, then what are you?"

With all my structures removed, I felt very uncomfortable. They're my marker buoys, my navigation aids. I used to accuse Paul of treating me like a collection of services. The weird thing was I didn't know who I was when all those services were taken away. To the question, "What defines you?" I had to answer, "My roles do."

The months that I labored on this book took me away from my usual family obligations. "I'm neglecting everything," I lamented to Paul after a few weeks. "The kids, the cooking, the house. I feel so guilty. What kind of mother am I?"

"It's true things aren't functioning as well without you," he said. "But what kind of mother will you be if you never finish this book?"

I considered that for a minute.

"Disappointed. Unhappy," I answered. "Full of regrets."

"There's your answer," he said. "Now get back to work."

The familiar and well-rehearsed had a strong pull on me. My knee-jerk reactions may have also had another motivation.

"What's all this guilt helping you to avoid?" Stephanie asked pointedly.

"Uh, the hard work of writing," I sheepishly confessed. I'd rather sell a lung than sit down at the computer and create. It's not simple or straightforward. Organizing my life around others was so much easier.

Writing this chapter forced me to break brush on the "me"

trail, and it was difficult. If I'm not roles, services, relationships, or definitions, what am I? The answer lies in that vast uncharted wilderness that echoes back just one intimidating phrase:

"Anything you want."

Afterword

The Shortest Distance Between Two People is a Story.

After reading a book about military spouses during deployments, I flipped it over and glanced at the back copy. Negative words like "suffering," "anguish," "hardship," and "burdens" jumped out at me.

While no doubt military life is a challenging path, it offers unique rewards as well. There is the joy of camaraderie, community, and service. The opportunities for personal growth have given me a rich and satisfying expedition of self-discovery. I've learned that humor can get us through just about anything. When someone says "I know just how you feel," it helps navigate the rough spots.

Do you have a story to share? I invite you to contribute to an exciting upcoming project. *Household Claims* is a planned anthology of essays for military wives, by military wives. Its purpose is to enlighten, uplift, and entertain.

You'll find complete submission guidelines at my website, www.HouseholdBaggage.com. You can also order books, download reading club discussion questions, and request signed book plates. I look forward to hearing from you.

Be well and stay in touch,
Marna Krajeski
Marna@HouseholdBaggage.com

Glossary of Military Terms

Accompanied Tour—Tour of duty with family members.

Active Duty—When the military is your full-time job.

Air Assault—An attack using helicopters to insert troops and equipment.

Alert—An emergency call to be ready.

Assignment—Job/unit while on active duty.

BDU—Battle Dress Uniform, the leafy green camouflage print that replaced fatigues. In the desert, soldiers wear the Desert Camouflage Uniform (DCU). Both are being replaced by the Army Combat Uniform (ACU), which can be used in either place.

Battalion—A unit of 500 to 900 soldiers.

Chain of Command—The leadership structure in the military.

Chaplain—Military minister, priest, rabbi, imam, or pastor.

Class A's—The Army uniform that looks like a green business suit with all the ribbons and badges on the front.

Class B's—Class A green pants and shirt but no jacket, although a tie may be worn.

Colors—United States flag and unit/organization flags.

Commander—The person in charge of a unit.

Commissary—Grocery store for military members and their families.

Company—A unit of up to 200 soldiers.

Deployment—A mission without family members.

DCU—Desert Camouflage Uniform.

Dining Facility—The place where soldiers eat meals. It used to be called a mess hall.

Dining In—Formal social gathering for military members only.

Dining Out—Formal social gathering for military members and guests.

Discharge—Departure from active duty.

DOD—Department of Defense.

DONSA—"Day of No Scheduled Activity" on the calendar. It used to be called a training holiday.

Exchange—The retail store on a military installation. An Army post has a Post Exchange (PX); the Navy has a Naval Exchange (NEX); the Air Force has a Base Exchange (BX).

Field—The woods or other training site.

FTX—Field Training Exercise.

Hail and Farewell—An informal get-together to welcome new people and say goodbye to others.

High and Tight—A severe military haircut with very short sides and little hair on top.

Household Baggage—Furniture and belongings in a moving van; also known as Household Goods.

Household 6—The suffix "6" designates the commander, so this is the person in charge of the house (not an official title).

Infantry—Riflemen or foot soldiers in the Army.

Leave—Approved time away from duty. Known as vacation time to civilians.

Leave and Earnings Statement (LES)—A pay stub.

MP—Military Police.

MRE—Meals, Ready-to-Eat. Food that replaced C-Rations.

MWR—An agency dedicated to morale, welfare, and recreation.

Master Blaster—The top paratrooper award.

NCO—Non-commissioned officer. An enlisted person who has been promoted to the rank of corporal or sergeant and above.

NTC—The National Training Center, a desert training site at Ft. Irwin, California.

Non-Appropriated Fund—Non-tax dollars spent on military facilities.

Orders—Official paperwork assigning a soldier somewhere.

Protocol—Customs and courtesies.

PCS—Permanent Change of Station, i.e. moving.

POV—Privately Owned Vehicle, i.e. a car.

PT—Physical Training. What soldiers do to stay in shape, such as running and push-ups.

PX—See "Exchange."

Platoon—A unit of sixteen to forty soldiers.

Post—An Army installation. If it's Air Force or Navy property, it's called a "base."

Quarters—Government housing.

ROTC—Reserve Officers' Training Corps or Military Science at a university.

Rations—Food for soldiers.

Rank—Official title of a military person.

Rear Detachment—The commander's representatives who do not deploy with the unit but have responsibilities at the home station.

Reserve Component—Army and Air National Guard and the US Army Reserves.

Road March—Physical conditioning which involves carrying rucksacks and walking at an accelerated pace.

Rucksack—A large military-issued back pack.

Shoppette—The convenience store on post.

TDY—Temporary Duty. The military equivalent of a business trip. It could be a day or six months, but it's temporary, as opposed to PCS, which is permanent (but not really).

Unaccompanied Tour—An assignment without family members.

Gratitude

The biggest thanks go to my husband Paul: first editor, military fact checker, and one-man cheering squad. I love you. Hugs to Elena and Stephen, my tickets to the human race and my two greatest teachers.

My parents actively encouraged me over the years, as did Paul's. Both fathers served in the Air Force, and my mother, mother-in-law, and stepmother have all been military wives themselves.

Colleagues in the College Writing Program at the University of Rhode Island unselfishly provided expert feedback, in particular Dr. Nedra Reynolds, Karen Ruhren, Lisa Magnuson, Susan Rashid Horn, Mary Angel Blount, and Dr. Libby Miles. Kudos also to the helpful staff at the URI library where a good portion of this book was written.

The Austin Peay State University crowd got me through graduate school and made the Fort Campbell years so much fun, especially Dr. Jill Eichhorn, Barry Kitterman, and Dr. Michael Schnell.

The Writers' Groups at the Narragansett Library, Barnes and Noble in Middletown, and the Cross Mills Library all had a hand in shaping this book.

Bob Gulla, editor extraordinaire, came through for me.

Lieutenant Colonel Dave Jones is the gifted cartoonist responsible for the illustrations.

Marcia Yudkin (Yudkin.com) helped me refine the proposal. Rosemary Daniell got me writing in the first place with her example (Myzonarosa.com). Bonnie Leonard, a former Navy wife, is a wealth of information (Compasswise.com). Stephanie Marisca Straight offered guidance on the cover, and the Dwyers never failed to ask about my progress. Thanks to all of you.

Nancy Cleary of Wyatt-MacKenzie Publishing and the gang at the Mom Writers Publishing Co-op shine as a creative team.

The Association of Graduates at the US Military Academy believed in me enough to let me write "Gray Matter." Many thanks Tom Mulyca.

Michael and Kathy Derrick have kept us company on the journey from the start. Andy and Lisa Glen provide welcome hospitality whenever we are at West Point. Forever Friends Aimee, Angela, Ellen, Kathy, Kelly, Maris, Robin, Sheila, Theresa, and others make life sweeter.

Salutes to military wives the world over for their sisterhood and colorful inspiration!

Publishing the Works of Extraordinary Mom Writers

Wyatt-MacKenzie Publishing, Inc

WyMacPublishing.com